Winnifred
E. Short
Memorial

J. Morehouse

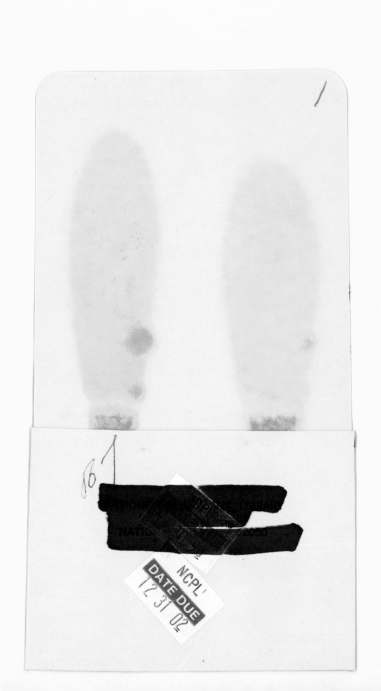

THE LAST OF
THE SCOTTSBORO BOYS

THE LAST OF
THE SCOTTSBORO
BOYS

An Autobiography by

Clarence Norris

and

Sybil D. Washington

G. P. PUTNAM'S SONS
NEW YORK

Library of Congress Cataloging in Publication Data

Norris, Clarence.
  The last of the Scottsboro boys.

  1. Norris, Clarence. 2. Scottsboro Case.
3. Afro-Americans—Alabama—Biography. 4. Alabama—
Biography. I. Washington, Sybil D., joint author.
II. Title.
E185.93.A3N676 1978   976.1'06'0924 [B]   78-23428
ISBN 0-399-12018-1

Printed in the United States of America

ACKNOWLEDGMENTS

Acknowledgments are due the many people who made this book a reality. Our thanks to: Dr. Dan T. Carter, professor emeritus, Department of History, Emory University, Atlanta, Georgia; William and Louise Patterson of the International Labor Defense; James Meyerson, counsel for the National Association for the Advancement of Colored People; Clinton "Slim" Brown of the Alabama Department of Archives and History. Special thanks for time spared me from their busy schedules for interviews and consultation are due to: William J. Baxley, attorney general of Alabama; Milton C. Davis, an assistant attorney general; and Alvin Holmes, a member of the Alabama legislature. Linda Amster of the New York *Times,* Mamie Dixon, and James Hairston provided much help.

For my people
and in loving memory of Ida Norris,
my mother.
——CLARENCE NORRIS

PREFACE

To me the history of Black America is embodied in the life saga of Clarence Norris, the victim of circumstances beyond his control dictated by one factor—the color of his skin. The punishment meted out in Alabama to him and the eight other black teenagers he was with was revenge for their audacity in fighting back when provoked by other hobos (white) as all were traveling on a freight train in 1931 during the Depression era. When two frightened, destitute white women also aboard the train swore that they were raped by these black youths, Alabama governors, judges, prosecutors and other elected officials seized the opportunity to capitalize politically on the ensuing publicity. Despite clinical evidence, common sense and decency, the nine were denied their freedom for a total of one hundred and four years. Norris underwent the torture of numerous dates of execution and languished on death row for five years. Finally, when his sentence was commuted to life, he spent an additional ten years in prison.

The decades between 1931 and the present day have spanned much social change for blacks, particularly in the Southern states. On November 29, 1976, the state of Alabama granted Clarence Norris an unconditional pardon based on the decision that he was innocent. On the basis of the same "evidence" on which the Scottsboro

9

Boys were convicted more than forty years ago, Alabama at last admitted that it would have killed nine innocent youths. In Alabama today there are over four hundred thousand blacks in a total electorate of a million six hundred thousand. I believe this was a significant factor in granting the pardon. Unfortunately, the other Scottsboro Boys are dead, so they never will enjoy the knowledge of their vindication.

Mr. Norris is a true hero in the sense that in his fight for freedom and dignity, two landmark decisions were handed down by the United States Supreme Court to the advantage of all Americans. Upon meeting him I found a happy man, enjoying life and looking fifteen years younger than his age of sixty-four. An uneducated but highly intelligent man, robust, strong, a survivor, devoid of bitterness and hatred.

He told me that he had waited for the right time to tell of his experiences and agreed to collaborate with me on the book. Over a period of months I taped interviews with him and analyzed and edited the transcripts. I examined documents in the Library of Congress, Boston University, Cornell University, the United States Supreme Court library and the Alabama Department of Archives and History. I spent two months in Chattanooga, Tennessee, home of four of the Scottsboro defendants. From that vantage point I visited the Alabama localities of Scottsboro, Decatur, Huntsville and Birmingham to interview principals in the case and peruse newspaper files. From the collaborative effort with Mr. Norris and from my own research, a balanced and full account of the Scottsboro Case emerges.

—SYBIL D. WASHINGTON

CONTENTS

11

From the New York *Times*——October 26, 1976

Quotation of the Day
"The lesson to black people, to my children, to everybody is that you should always fight for your rights, even
if it cost you your life. Stand up for your rights, even if it
kills you. That's all that life consists of."
—CLARENCE NORRIS, the sole surviving "Scottsboro Boy,"
who was pardoned by the State of Alabama.

THE LAST OF
THE SCOTTSBORO BOYS

CHAPTER ONE

A Legal Lynching

Those were desperate times in the late nineteen twenties, the beginning of the Great Depression. Make no doubt, the Southern Negro was hit the hardest. It was tough to survive it all. Myself and thousands of others stole rides on freight trains and rode from city to city and town to town in search of work. It was against the law to hop those trains but the jails couldn't hold all the folks doing it, so the railroad detectives didn't pay us no mind.

There was no money. A loaf of bread was five cents, a can of sardines, five cents, big juicy hamburgers cost a dime, but I couldn't buy none of it. Oh, there were bread lines and soup lines, but they were segregated. When the government started giving out flour, beans and staples to the poor people, Negroes risked their lives to try and get the relief because white folks thought they should have it all.

I went to strangers' homes and begged for food. I offered to do any kind of work for a meal. After being in a town all day scrounging around, I slept in the hobo jungles. They were always near the railroads, under bridges or in the woods. They would be packed with men talking of their troubles and everybody telling their story. We built bonfires to stay warm through the nights and to cook whatever food we had. Rumors were always flying, about where jobs might be and sometimes I lucked up.

I remember the last job I got before I was arrested. Help was needed to dig the foundation for a building. There was close to fifty men lined up who wanted the work. The pay was twenty cents an hour. The boss went down the line and picked the biggest, healthiest-looking men. The men not hired stood around waiting. They knew somebody would quit or be fired, 'cause they was working us like mules. We were using picks and shovels. The foreman come around to me and said, "Every time the man next to you brings up a shovelful, you bring up a shovelful." After an hour of this my pace slowed some, here come the boss: "Keep up now, I got a bunch of fellas to take your place." I threw down the tools and told him they could have my place. And they wouldn't give me my twenty cents!

There was lots of rackets concerning work back then. I'd be hired for a job and when I was through the man wouldn't pay me what he had said and I might not get nothing. You could be walking down the street and the cops would pick you up for vagrancy 'cause you didn't have a job. Then you'd end up on a chain gang in a quarry, picking crops, building roads: free labor.

It was March 25, 1931, when I caught a train out of Chattanooga, Tennessee, headed for Memphis. The train

18

was a main line southern that went from Tennessee to Georgia and Alabama, then back into Tennessee. As the train went along more and more hobos jumped aboard, black men and white men. I had been riding for some time when the whites started throwing gravel at the blacks, talking about "All you niggers unload, get your asses offa here."

They had to be crazy. We were out in the middle of nowhere, all of us stealing a ride, and these crackers start acting like they owned the train. I wasn't getting off and some of the other black guys must have felt the same way. We fought the white boys, and it was a bloody battle too. We beat the hell out of them and made 'em get off the train. The ones that didn't want to go we throwed off. We were moving pretty fast, so when they hit the ground they would tumble quite a ways. We let one guy stay because the train started moving too fast for him to make a safe landing. We had really put it to them but they had brought it on themselves. After the fight I went back to where I had been sitting on a cross-tie car.

Every now and then the train had to stop and take on water. I didn't think nothing of it when we stopped at a little place, a flag station, Paint Rock, Alabama. But when I looked up, the tracks were lined with a mob of men. They had sticks, pistols, rifles, shotguns; everything you need to murder, they had it. The fellas we had throwed off the train were there too. The mob circled the train and made us all get off. They pushed and shoved us until we were lined up in front of a building. We were surrounded by a sea of white faces, screaming, "Let's hang these black sons of bitches. Where's the rope for these niggers?"

Two men had on uniforms. I don't know if they were police, firemen or soldiers, but they saved our lives. They asked the white boys who it was had been in the fight. The white boys answered we were all in it. The men in uniform said, "Let's take them to jail." Somebody drove up in a school bus. They put handcuffs on us nine Negroes that had been taken off and ran a rope through the handcuffs so we were connected. They put us on the bus and all the whites that could get on packed in too. We were taken to the nearest jail, in Scottsboro, Alabama. That's why we are called the Scottsboro Boys today.

They put the nine of us in a large cage by ourselves, and they locked those white hobos up somewhere in there too. This is where I made the acquaintance of the rest of the Scottsboro Boys. There were four out of Chattanooga that were friends—two brothers, Roy and Andy Wright, and Eugene Williams and Haywood Patterson. Ozie Powell, Olen Montgomery, Charlie Weems, Willie Roberson and myself were all from different parts of Georgia.

Olen Montgomery was almost blind, couldn't hardly see nothing, and he walked with a stick. Willie Roberson was real bad off. He was so sick he could hardly move. He had syphilis and his privates was swole up to twice their size. He had sores all over him too. Neither one of these boys was in the fight.

All of us were scared to death, quite natural, and we didn't know what was going to happen next. Late that evening crackers were outside the jail, hollering and screaming and cursing us. They told the sheriff to "bring those niggers out." They said they would come in and get us if we weren't released. When they crowded into

20

the doorway the sheriff pulled his gun. He said, "If you come in here I will blow your brains out. Get away from here." You never heard such a racket then. That made them mad as hell. The sheriff turned off the lights; he wanted to move us but it was too late. The jail was surrounded. The deputies kept telling the sheriff to move us but he knew we didn't stand a chance on the street. The crowd was howling like dogs, throwing rocks and threatening to burn us out.

The sheriff called Governor Ben Miller and asked him to send in the National Guard. The governor didn't waste any time. It wasn't long before I heard the Guard outside. They had to put something on those crackers; they cracked some heads because they wouldn't leave peaceable. After the Guard cleared the streets, they stationed themselves outside the jail and all over town. But I didn't get any sleep that night.

Next day we were taken from the cage and put in a line. The sheriff brought two women over to us. He said, "Miss Price, which one of these niggers had you?" She went down the line pointing her finger: "This one, this one, this one . . . until she had picked out six, including me. They asked the other woman, Ruby Bates, the same question but she did not part her lips. A guard said, "Well, if those six had Miss Price it stands to reason the others had Miss Bates." We all started talking at once: "We never did any such thing"; "No, sheriff, we didn't do that." I blurted out that it was a lie. Before I could blink that guard struck out at me with his bayonet. I threw up my hands and he slashed my right hand open to the bone. He screamed, "Nigger, you know damn well how to talk about white women."

They shoved us back into the cage. I was scared be-

21

fore, but it wasn't nothing to how I felt now. I knew if a white woman accused a black man of rape, he was as good as dead. My hand was bleeding like I don't know what, my blood was running out of me like water. I tore my shirt and wrapped the rag around my hand real tight. I bled for a long time before it stopped that day but I didn't even think about it. All I could think was that I was going to die for something I had not done. I had never seen those two women before in my life.

It was all the National Guard could do to keep the crowds back now. They were getting bigger all the time. The sheriff took us to Gadsden, Alabama, for safekeeping. The Guard was with us every step of the way or we never would have made it. We stayed in Gadsden until we went to trial in Scottsboro.

We went to trial on April 6, 1931. The Interdenominational Ministers Alliance, a group of black preachers in Chattanooga, raised fifty dollars to hire us a lawyer. He came to see us about half an hour before the trial. He was a white man named Stephen Roddy. He looked us over and asked us which ones did the raping. He said, "Now if you boys will tell the truth, I might be able to save some of your lives." I didn't know what a lawyer was supposed to be but I knew this one was no good for us. He had liquor on his breath and he was as scared as we were. When we got into the courtroom and the judge asked him if he was our lawyer, the man said, "Not exactly."

The walk from the jail to the courthouse seemed a hundred miles. The crowd was thick as hair on a dog's back. There were thousands of people in Scottsboro that day. It was like a holiday. Bands were playing and food and drinks were being sold in the streets. The National Guardsmen were everywhere, and they put their bodies between us and the mob. As soon as the crowd saw us, they started screaming, "You niggers gonna die. Your black asses gonna burn. The electric chair's too good for you bastards." Such as that. There wasn't a black face to be seen. The courtroom was jammed, full up. The ones who couldn't get a seat were standing up and leaning against the walls.

The trials lasted for three days. There were four trials for nine men. I don't know how they decided we should be tried. Charlie Weems and me went first, then Haywood Patterson was tried by himself. Olen Montgomery, Ozie Powell, Willie Roberson, Andy Wright and Eugene Williams were all tried together. Roy Wright went last.

I truly can't remember much of those trials. The judge was Alfred E. Hawkins and he was a low-down bastard. He let it be known he thought we were guilty and a trial was a waste of time and money "for niggers." I was nervous, confused and scared. Outside the crowds were whooping it up, and inside the courtroom they were jumping up and down, waving guns and laughing.

I know those women took the stand and testified under oath. They put their hands on the Bible and lied and lied. They said we raped them on a bed of gravel in an open freight car. They said we used knives and hit them up the side of the head with guns to make them have sex. But the law never found no knives or guns on us because we didn't have any.

Two doctors were witnesses. Their testimony was that they had examined the women after they said they were raped. The examination took place about a half an hour afterwards. They said they found semen in the women but not very much. Also they didn't have any wounds or fresh bruises.

All of us got the death penalty except Roy Wright. He looked so young the state didn't ask for the death of him, just life imprisonment. But his jury was divided on whether to kill him or not. So his was declared a mistrial. He was never tried again but they kept him at Birmingham in the Jefferson County Jail for six years until he was released in 1937. He was thirteen years old.

Judge Hawkins sentenced us to die April 9, 1931. The eight of us stood before him. He asked us if we had anything to say. None of us spoke. He said, ". . . it is the judgment of the court and the sentence of the law that the defendants be sentenced to death by electrocution at Kilby Prison in the City of Montgomery, Montgomery County, Alabama, on Friday the 10th day of July, 1931." I was eighteen, also Charlie Weems and Olen Montgomery; Haywood Patterson and Andy Wright were nineteen; Ozie Powell was fifteen; Willie Roberson was fourteen, and Eugene Williams was thirteen years old.

I never saw so many happy white folks. They went wild. Cheers went up all over town. They were rejoicing over our fate. There was dancing in the streets. The bands played "There'll be a Hot Time in the Old Town Tonight."

We were rushed back to the jail in Gadsden. This time we were put in a big cage with about ten other black prisoners. Up till then we had some small hope, but now we knew for sure what lay in store for us. We talked it over and decided to make a break instead of waiting to be executed. We cursed the guards and told them to bring us food. We shouted and banged on the bars. One

24

guard brought us some cold biscuits. We threw them down and stomped on them. We called him dirty names and demanded he bring us some hot meals. We wanted him to have to open the cell door. He walked over to the cage and said, "You goddamn niggers, cool off." He was close enough for me and Haywood to grab him. We struggled with him, trying to get his gun and keys. He was screaming his head off and in seconds the place was full of the guards. They opened the cage with their guns on us. They said, "All you niggers not in the rape case walk out." Then they handcuffed the eight of us in couples. They beat us damn near to death. They kicked, punched and stomped us till they got tired.

There was no sleeping that night. We were a bloody mess. I was handcuffed to Ozie Powell. They kept us like that all the next day and we got nothing to eat or drink. At dusk dark a truck came for us. The sheriff ran a length of chain through our handcuffs. The sheriff and the National Guard took us to the Jefferson County Jail in Birmingham. The National Guard was let go after they got us there.

Jefferson County Jail was much bigger than the other places we had been. It was new and made out of big stones and brick. We were put into separate cells. They treated us real tough there because we had tried to escape.

The other prisoners told us we were famous. The newspaper reporters came from all over to see us. Every day we got sacks of mail. People sent us money, cigarettes and candy. The guards there didn't like this at all. They wouldn't let anybody that would do us some good get in to see us. Some of the boys' relatives tried to visit them but were turned away.

Days rocked around and two men came to see us. They told the guards they had come from Tuscaloosa, Alabama, to see those "Scottsboro niggers." They looked like farmers and talked like rednecks. I thought they had come to torment us when they put us in a room with them. These men were Joseph R. Brodsky and Allan Taub from New York City, two white lawyers. They said they were with the International Labor Defense [ILD]. They told us not to worry about going to the chair. Mr. Brodsky and Mr. Taub made us feel a lot better when they said hundreds of people were working to get us free. They asked us if we wanted them to be our lawyers. These men brought us the first kind words from the outside world since we had been arrested. I had never met white men like them. They really seemed to care what happened to us all. If those deputies had known what Brodsky and Taub were telling us they would have killed them. The one thing those rednecks hate worse than a nigger is a nigger-lover. We told the lawyers we wanted all the help we could get and all they could give us.

We had been in Birmingham several weeks when one night the high sheriff of Jefferson County came to take us to the death house in Kilby Prison.

CHAPTER TWO

Youth

I was born in Warm Springs, Georgia, in the country on a farm. My mother and daddy had eleven children, four boys and seven girls. All but two lived, a boy was born dead and my sister Reeche died of dysentery in my mother's arms. My brother Willie was older than me by five years, then came Lucille, Blanche, Inez, my brother Port, Ina Mae, Ida Belle (she never let nobody call her anything but Virginia) and Ebeneezer. We grew up like stairsteps.

The family lived in different towns in Georgia, all within walking distance of each other. We sharecropped in Warm Springs, Molena and Neal, moving from farm to farm. My daddy never owned any land, so he was in the control of the white man. They would provide him with a house to live in and so many acres of land to grow crops, mostly cotton. At the end of the year the white man would sell the crop and give my daddy a share of the profits, after he had taken out the money for the seed, fertilizer and any other necessities my daddy had to get from him before the crop was sold.

My daddy put me in the fields to work when I was six or seven years old. My mother worked in the fields and all of the children too, as soon as they got some size. I never liked farming. I didn't like putting a sack around my neck, stooping down to pick cotton, chop cotton and ramming it in the sack under the hot sun. By the time I was ten I was pulling cotton, plowing and planting; everything a grown man could do I did or my daddy would whup me good. He was a hard taskmaster and he would beat us at the drop of a hat. He was rough on all of us but I guess he didn't know any other way. I never could go to school but a couple of days out of a week. I didn't go past the second grade. You didn't bite my daddy's bread and go to school after a certain age. So none of us children got an education.

I never knew much about my father's people. I know he was part Indian. He was a tall, handsome man and he was a great deal older than my mother. He had long straight black hair down to his waist, and his skin was a bright copper color. He always wore his hair in two thick braids. He had teeth as white as snow and they were like that when he died. Not a spoiled tooth in his head.

My daddy had been a slave, and he would tell us about his life back then. He had a finger missing, the same one I was to lose in the penitentiary. My daddy said one of his masters chopped that finger off with an ax because he was late getting up one morning.

My daddy had a sister name of Hattie. One day they were in the fields and the white overseer jumped on Hattie. She fought him and beat him good. She walked away to go to the master's house; the overseer got up and split her head wide open with a hoe. She died on the spot. As a small boy my father talked to me of many things, but after I got some size, me and him didn't have much conversation. All he talked about was the work to be done. He was a hard man but he did the work of ten men, stayed with his family and we never went hungry.

The sweetest life I have ever lived is the country life. The South is a beautiful part of the world. I liked the fresh air, the birds singing everywhere and the animals. The flowers made the air smell so sweet and it was peaceful and quiet. There was lots of water: lakes, rivers, streams and creeks.

My mother loved to fish, and she took me with her from the time I was very young. We fished night and day. We'd go in the early morning before the sun was up and set out as many as fifty lines. In the evening we would go around to all the hooks to see as to our success. We caught catfish, perch and eels, mostly. We always brought our fish home to clean. We never did that on the banks of the river.

There were times when white and black families would go seining together. The law put a stop to this kind of fishing because you caught too many. The men brought big nets that stretched from one side of the river to the other. Men on each of the river banks caught hold of the nets and dragged them through the water until they were full. Then they divided up the catch.

The women would cook the fish right there on the river bank. We'd have a feast with all the cakes, pies, homemade bread, lemonade and other good eats the families had brought. Blankets were spread on the grassy slopes and we ate until we were fit to bust. Those were good times.

29

As I grew older my father took me hunting, which was something I loved to do. We hunted squirrels, rabbits, possum, coon and birds. There was no end to the birds: partridges, doves, quail—so many I can't name them all. I was pretty good with a shotgun but I couldn't ever handle a rifle too well. We hunted rabbits in the wet places where something grew that we called cane. It wasn't sugar cane but it looked like it. People made fishing poles out of it. Some rabbits lived on the high land and were called sage rabbits. They didn't get as large as the swamp rabbits that could hit fifteen pounds.

We went possum hunting at night and we had to use dogs. The dogs would tree the possum for us. We used torches to find them on the tree branches. If the tree had plenty of branches we would climb up and grab the possum by the neck. I had to be careful because a possum will bite you seriously. If we couldn't climb the tree we shot them down.

Although my daddy raised a cash crop such as cotton, wheat or corn for whoever he was sharecropping, we always had a large garden of our own. We grew collards, mustards, turnips, tomatoes, corn, beans, okra, cabbages, potatoes and yams. At the end of summer my mother would be canning for weeks to put up for the winter months. We never had a worry about food.

We always had four or five cows giving milk and we raised hogs too. My brothers and me took turns milking the cows every morning. My mother made her own butter, with a churn she rocked with her foot.

Every year my daddy would put the hogs he planned to kill in a pen that had a wooden floor. This way they couldn't get to no filth. We cleaned them out and fattened them up on corn, wheat and fodder for four or five months. After hog killing time the smokehouse would be full of smoked meats and sausages. What people call chitterlings today is what was used as the skin of the sausages; we ground our own. The slaughterhouses gave that part away along with the ears, liver, lights, feet, tails, snouts, brains and hearts of the hog. My family went and got all we wanted. Just about all parts of the hog is good eating.

I remember when my mother and daddy bought us children a billy goat. He was a pretty little thing with an all white body except for a brown spot on his face. The little goat ate anything we gave him. When he got older my mother bought a wagon and a harness. We hitched up Billy and he would ride us all around the property. But that goat got so big and bad we couldn't do a thing with him. He had both my legs covered with sores because of his butting and fighting with me. When he got mad the hair would stand up straight, all over his body. He got so bad that when my mother would hang clothes on the line, he would tear them down and chew them up. Mother started talking about getting rid of the goat. He would come into the kitchen and get up on the table. He got so he ran my mother and sisters out of the house. Everyone in the family had been knocked down more than once by him. Finally he bristled up at my daddy and he got his shotgun to kill Billy, but mother wouldn't let him. All us children begged and pleaded for the goat's life. So my daddy sold him to a white man who wanted Billy for his son. A few weeks later we learned the man had killed Billy.

When I was a kid it was horse-and-buggy days. My daddy bought a fine red horse and a brand-new rubber-tired buggy. You were a big shot if you had one of those buggies. My mother fussed because after he bought the horse and buggy he would be gone days at a time. We all loved the horse, Tom, and the new buggy, and we went to town, church and all over the county visiting relatives in it. My big brother Willie did his first courting with that buggy. One day my daddy sent me and Willie to the pasture to get Tom. We walked all over but we couldn't find him. Later daddy found Tom in a stream, shot through the head and all his legs broke. My daddy beat me and Willie unmerciful but we hadn't done nothing to the horse.

The next day the white man we were sharecropping for left a note on the porch. It said, "Your children didn't kill your horse, I did and I've my shotgun loaded to kill you on sight." Daddy left us then and said he would send for us as soon as he could. He said he would be in Neal, Georgia. I never knew why the man was so mad at my daddy he killed his horse. We were living in Warm Springs at the time. In about four months he sent for us, and we moved to Neal to start sharecropping way up in the mountains.

We stayed there a good while. I became real good friends with a boy they called R. L. but his name was Robert Lee. I spent many happy hours with his family. R. L. had fifteen sisters and one brother. I called myself, courting two of his sisters, Alice and Gladys. I talked to them and held their hands but there was mighty few times I could get a kiss.

We moved from there because the man who owned the property got hot for my momma. This low snake came to the house when my daddy was away. He always asked for a cup of coffee or something to eat, and my mother would fix it for him. Finally he grabbed her one day and was tussling with her till he drug her into another room and slammed the door. All us children was there and we busted through the door. He had momma on the floor, tearing her clothes and forcing hisself on top of her. We commenced screaming and hollering to beat the band. He left. White people could pull some rotten tricks on black folks 'cause they knew the law was always on their side. My daddy came home and we packed up that very day. We moved to Mr. Watt's place in Molena, Georgia.

One day Willie and me were walking along the highway. There wasn't many cars in those days and we had never ridden in one. Two white boys came driving up and asked us if we wanted to ride. Quite naturally we did. The car had running boards on each side. I got on one and Willie got on the other. We were holding onto the door handles. The driver took off like a shot, zigzagging across this bumpy road trying to throw us off. I was hanging on for dear life. We begged them to stop. They laughed at us. I jumped off and so did my brother. We tumbled over the gravel and got badly bruised. These white fellas thought it was the funniest thing.

I have had grown white men shoot bullets around the feet of me and my playmates when we were in the town. This was to make us dance for them. And they made us dance until we dropped. Our parents taught us to avoid whites and stay out of their path because you never knew what might happen.

I began to hate my daddy on account of what some white man said and it was a lie. This white man had about seventy-five beehives in a pine thicket. Somebody came along and set the woods on fire, so the beehives burnt up. The man came to my daddy and told him my brother and me had set the fire. Daddy stripped us buck naked in front of this man and beat us like we was mules. I couldn't never love him after that, not from that day to this.

My mother's mother, Grandma Lucy, I loved very much. She lived in Denile, Georgia. She was a sweet woman and she thought the world of us children. She was our Santa Claus all year long. She told the very best ghost stories. She had me afraid to go out at night. She got so sick before she died, momma went to stay with her. We were all scared she would die. I ran away and went to see my momma and Grandmother Lucy. My grandma was in bed, but she looked the same and talked to me. My mother told me to go and find Dick Gamble, grandma's husband, because she wasn't going to last long. Dick Gamble and Grandma Lucy had been separated for some years. I ran all the way to Neal to find him. When we got back my mother was crying because her mother had just passed away. It was a strange experience for me; she was alive when I left the house and when I got back she was dead. I couldn't believe she'd never say anything to me again.

On Sunday everybody went to church in those little country towns. We belonged to Mount Olive Baptist Church in Neal. My daddy and grandmother are buried in the cemetery there. I was made to go to church after a certain age. I had to be forced. I was too restless to sit, and the services went on and on. I saw three of my sisters baptized there, but I never was. We got to church at nine in the morning for Sunday school and stayed most of the day. It was the only black church for miles around; there was always a big turn out. We took baskets of food and ate off tables set up under the trees.

I enjoyed the singing most of all. We made the little church sway from side to side. The old spirituals I still remember now, they are beautiful. The white people came to our church to hear the singing. The two front pews were always kept vacant for them. Of course it was understood we could never enter their churches.

There would be big revival meetings that lasted for weeks. Famous evangelists came through to save our souls. These were the big-time preachers. The women cooked and baked for days before these events. We had tables of food and everything was free. I would go from table to table, eating as much as I could. We went every day until it ended. Many souls were saved with lots of shouting, fainting and crying. Lots of folks were baptized the last week of these going-ons. In those days people were baptized in the river; the women wore long white dresses. It was an exciting time.

The men had jugs of corn liquor sitting off in the woods. I have set up all night watching my daddy make corn liquor. We had a still in the house and one in the woods. My daddy sold it for thirty cents a pint bottle. My daddy sold liquor as long as I can remember. Most folks that bought it from him were white. They would come at all times of the night. My brothers and sisters and me would sneak and drink it and get really loaded and of course whupped for it. My mother gave us tonics made of the liquor, sugar and water to ward off colds.

The house we had on Mr. Watt's place in Molena had eight rooms, a big front porch, back porch and a fenced-in yard with a garage. It was a fine house and sat on the edge of the highway. We were the first black family to live in the house.

Mr. Watt had a big white house right across the road.

He had two sons and two daughters. You couldn't keep them out of our house. One of his sons was my age, and he became my playmate. He took food from his house, ham, yams, whatever, and we'd go swimming, fishing and hunting together. He was crazy about me. His daddy didn't pay us no mind but his momma would tell him, "Don't get too close to that nigger." She made sure I heard her. They had an old automobile and his momma sent him to the store in it. He'd tell me to go down the highway and meet him 'cause his momma didn't want me in the car.

His name was George and his little brother was Zack. Their sisters' names were Dottie and Dumpling. Zack and my little brother Port were buddies. We called Port "Joe Rooster," and everybody called me "Bubba." They had the run of our house, but we never went as far as their back door. I never thought of this until later years. One day Joe Rooster jumped on Zack fit to kill. Zack had called him black—in those days that was a fighting word more so than nigger. George and me broke them up before the grown people heard it. My brother told Zack never to call him black again and Zack said he wouldn't.

We were in our teens when George come to me and said, "Bubba, momma wants you to call me Mr. George now. Call me that in front of her, but otherwise you don't have to do it." I got a funny feeling and I told him I didn't have to call him nothing. He said, "I want you to call me George, just plain George, but don't let momma hear you." Soon after we drifted apart.

I hated farming, so quite naturally my father and me didn't get along after I reached the teen years. I didn't want to be a sharecropper, to work hard all year doing

backbreaking work and lucky to end up with a new pair
of overalls. I wanted to leave the farm and find some
other work. I wanted to get my hands on my own
money. My daddy began to whup me almost daily. He'd
tie me to a tree and beat me with tree branches. My
momma would run out with a butcher knife and
threaten to kill him if he didn't stop. Even Mr. Watt told
him, "One day you are going to kill that boy."

The first time I left home I went down the road a
piece and got a job doing pretty much what I had done
at home, only I was getting eight dollars a week. I was
fifteen and big for my age. My daddy came on my job
and demanded my salary. I would not give it to him. He
said, "Come home, your mother is crying for you." I said
no.

Shortly after this, the year was 1928, my father collapsed with a heart attack on his way home from town.
Neighbors carried him home. Mr. Watt came by where I
was working and told me what had happened. I rushed
home and my mother and sisters were standing on the
porch crying; daddy had just passed on. There was no
such thing as an undertaker in so small a town. We
made our own dead ready for burial. The relatives took a
door and laid it across two chairs. They put a quilt on it
and a sheet. The body was bathed, dressed in his best
clothes and placed on the door, then he was covered up
to his neck with another sheet. Relatives and friends
came from all over and sat up with the body for two
nights. My father belonged to a lodge, and they ordered
a casket. When the casket came daddy was buried. I
didn't think I would cry, but when my mother cried so
much, my tears came but I don't know whether they
were for my daddy or my mother.

The neighbors and relatives helped momma to harvest the crop that year. My sister Blanche got married and she took the younger children in with her. My mother hired out to work for a white family. Willie was already married and gone. I went to Warm Springs to work at the resort there.

CHAPTER THREE

Early Travels

Warm Springs, Georgia, was the home of a big summer resort. Rich white people came from everywhere to enjoy themselves and soak in the warm mineral waters. It was on acres and acres of land. There was a hotel, clubhouse, golf courses, swimming pools and tennis courts. The black people of the town mostly depended on the resort for their livelihood. They worked there as cooks, waiters, chauffeurs, maids, caddies and gardeners.

I moved in with some cousins of mine. The family consisted of the mother, the father and their son Johnny. He was a fine boy, two years older than me. He worked in the clubhouse renting the bathing suits and lockers. The bosses thought the world of Johnny and he was able to get me a job at the resort.

I worked as a caddy during the day. The biggest part of my job was to keep my eye on the ball and carrying the golf clubs from one hole to the other. But I had to find that ball after it was hit. The women were the worst because they knocked it all over the place. In the evening I worked with another caddy everybody called Red because he was light-skinned. We cut the golf greens and the lawns. We used big hand mowers. We were allowed to swim in the pool on Wednesday evenings before we drained it, scrubbed it out and refilled it with fresh water. I enjoyed the work and the pay was good. I received thirty dollars every two weeks, plus tips.

I got my first experience gambling there. A group of us got together after work to play pitty-pat, then we advanced to Georgia skin. I lost most of the time at first 'cause I was green, but I really enjoyed cards and gambling.

One night when we finished work Red asked me did I want some ice cream. I said, "Yeah, but where you gonna get it?" He said, "Follow me." He was looking around over his shoulder as we walked to the clubhouse. There was a back window with a little hole in the pane. Red put a stick through the hole and lifted the latch on the window. It was clear he had done this before. There was ice cream, candy, golf balls, tennis balls, Coca-Cola and cigars. We ate and drank, then stuffed our pockets with candy, balls and we each took a box of cigars. Red kept saying, "Eat, take all you want, they never miss nothing." When we left I never thought about it no more.

A few weeks later Red and me was caddying and we both had finished nine holes. It was payday, we were walking around together. Red had some cigars stuck in his shirt pocket and he was puffing away on one. The boss came up on us. He said to Red, "Boy where did you get those cigars?" "I bought them," was Red's reply. The man said, "How much did you pay?" Red told him some

40

lie. The boss said, "Those cigars cost a dollar apiece. They are Havanas and I know you got them from the clubhouse store. Now we've been missing stuff and if you don't tell me the truth I'm going to call the law." Red confessed to the theft right away and said I was with him. The boss fired both of us and denied us our salaries. He left us with, "I don't know what-all you boys have taken from here, but I won't call the sheriff. Just get out."

I was so upset I wanted to kill Red. I cussed him to a fare-thee-well. He started crying 'cause his job was gone. He kept saying over and over, "What I'm gonna tell my momma?" I said he should have thought of that before he started smoking dollar cigars.

I went and told my cousin Johnny what had happened. He said, "Let's go to Birmingham. I've got some money saved and I'll get paid today." He was disgusted with his home life. He was nineteen years old. He told me he was sick and tired of his daddy taking all his money. His daddy had bought a car and wouldn't let Johnny drive it. That evening me, Johnny and two other boys left Warm Springs and headed for Birmingham. We hopped a freight train. We would get off at little towns to get something to eat, then we'd walk along the tracks until another train came along.

I had a real bad cold that kept getting worse. I was coughing up stuff that was yellow as gold. I couldn't eat, all I wanted was something cold to drink. I had fever, sweats, and I was getting weaker and weaker. When I couldn't walk no more I told them to go ahead and I would catch up with them.

There was a big empty house off the side of the road. The windows were all broke out and there was weeds around it taller than me. But there was a path through the weeds up to the house and around it. I walked onto the porch and fell dead out. I don't know how long I was out. I woke up freezing, so I crawled into the house and fell asleep on the bare boards. I woke up hot and thirsty. There was a stream near by. I staggered there and swallowed a bellyful of the water. It was cold and as clear as glass. A man came by and asked me what was the matter with me. I told him I was sick. He left saying he would be right back with food. I never saw him again. I went back to the house and lay on the porch. A man came down the path, he must have been going to work because he had a lunch bucket. He said, "Son, you surely look sick." He asked me when was the last time I ate. I told him I didn't know. He gave me everything out of his lunch bucket. I could only eat a little of this food. He said he had to get going to his job.

I said to myself, I've got to get home. I didn't know where I was and my mind was fuzzy. I got up and walked to the railroad tracks. I walked along them all day. I walked and walked until I could hardly lift a foot. I saw a house way across a field. A woman was sitting on the porch with two babies. I walked over there and practically fell into her lap. She grabbed me and carried me into the house. She laid me on a bed. Her husband came in, and they bathed me and gave me clean clothes. I don't know how many days I was in that bed. The woman made me hot soups and teas. These were some good black people. They told me no harm would come to me as long as I stayed there. They said I wasn't going nowhere until I got well. When I got better I helped out in the fields and they paid me fifty cents a day. After I was good and strong they gave me money to take the train and they told me to go home. They hitched up their wagon and drove me to the depot.

I went back to Johnny's house. His mother was happy to see me. She had gotten a letter from Johnny and he had told her how sick I had been. She had been worried about me. She said Johnny was in Boston working as a chauffeur. I visited my sisters in Molena and stayed with them a while. Somebody told me about a job in West Point, Georgia, working for a lumber company. I moved there and took the job.

I got a room in a boardinghouse owned by a big, black old single man. All his roomers were men. I had been there about a week when all the men that lived there went out. It was a Saturday night. I didn't know anybody in the town, so I went to bed early. I woke up to this man, the landlord, pulling on my privates. I jumped out of the bed. I was getting into my clothes and all the while the man was begging me to stay. He said I could have anything he had, if I would be nice to him. I got the hell out of there.

I went to another rooming house and slept on the porch until morning. Then I went in and asked to rent a room. I was able to move right in.

The next day the old man found out where I was staying and he came to the house. He told the people there I had stolen some of his clothes. I asked my landlady to come to my room and I had her look through my things. She told him there wasn't a piece there big enough for him to wear. She asked him to get out of her house and not to bother me again. He tried to start a rumor that I was a thief, but nobody believed the old nigger.

Time rocked around and I met a girl named Annie

Pearl. She was my landlady's niece. She was beautiful and I fell in love with her. I loved her better than anyone I have ever loved. She was a tall brown-skinned woman, two years older than me. I courted her and she taught me many things. She had some schooling, and she taught me how to add and to figure out what numbers were. We moved to Gadsden, Alabama, and rented a house. I found work at the Goodyear plant that was going up there. Goodyear was building a plant, plus five hundred houses for the people who would work there. My job was helping to build the fireplaces for the houses. They were really rushing to get this place finished, so I was able to work overtime a lot. I was making good money, working twelve and sixteen hours a day.

Me and Annie Pearl got along good for a time. I bought brand-new furniture for the house. I got a bedroom set, a living room set, dining room set and a stove and ice box on time. I paid twenty-five dollars down and five dollars a month. She fixed the place up real pretty, and I was as happy as I have ever been. We had been together for almost a year when she fell in love with someone else. She left me and moved in with him.

I was so downhearted I wanted to kill her and myself. I couldn't eat or sleep. I kept thinking how to get her back. I convinced her to step out with me one night. I asked her to come back to me, but there was no talking her into it. I had murder within my heart. We were walking across a bridge. I'll never forget that night. The moon was shining as bright as day. I was going to throw her off the bridge. She looked up at me and said, "Are you going to kill me, Bubba?" I ran away from her and never looked back. I left the house and the furniture that very night. I went to hoboing and riding the rails.

One night I landed in Birmingham. I didn't know my way around and I was tired and sleepy. There was some empty freight cars full of hay in the railroad yard. Watermelons had been in them 'cause I could smell them. I decided to crawl up on the hay to go to sleep. Some cops must have seen me. No sooner as I was falling off to sleep, I heard them talking: "I think he went up in this one. No maybe this one." They were searching for me. I buried myself in the hay. But finally I could hear them getting closer and closer until they were poking in the straw where I was. "Get outta there, nigger. What do you think you are doing?" I tried to explain myself. But they didn't want to hear nothing. They already had their guns out and they started hitting me as soon as I opened my mouth. One said, "We are going to give you a chance to run for your life." Of course I realized their intention was to shoot me. There was a tall wide signboard with weeds seven feet high behind it a few yards from where I was standing. I dived into the weeds under the signboard. Then I streaked on all fours through those weeds. I could hear the shots. I didn't come out of the weeds until I was far ahead of them. I was lucky enough to get away. When I looked around me I was in a white neighborhood. I could tell because there were big, fine houses up and down the street. I went up under a house and fell asleep. When I woke the sun was high. I was scared to come out, because I knew if somebody saw me I would be in more trouble. But I made it to the street before anybody saw me come from under the house. I made it out of the area and back to the railroad yards.

It was a hard shift hoboing. Sometimes I didn't eat for days. You had to be careful or you'd be arrested for vagrancy, put in jail for late hours. Especially the blacks.

The judges gave you thirty days and you might never get out. You could end up on a chain gang. Busting rocks for streets and highways; digging ditches for pipe. There were so many wanderers: youngsters and old people. Free labor. Some people were glad to go to jail, at the least they could eat. I was arrested for late hours and got ten days. I was sentenced to hard labor working in a quarry for the city.

There was a man in there with me whose story I have never forgotten. He was from the North. He was driving through Georgia with his white wife. The police stopped him and wanted to know why she was in the front seat with him. When they explained they were married, it was like waving a red flag in front of an angry bull. They got the hell beat out of them. Both of them were arrested after an unmerciful beating. He had been in there for over a year when I met him. He didn't know what had happened to his wife.

Lots of folks were locked up on trumped-up charges. In those days the cracker had license to do what he wanted to anybody. There wasn't no money anywhere and no jobs to be found. The hobos were called black-birds because they jumped on the trains in flocks. People were doing things in those days they never would have done. The prostitutes were like flies. White women, black women, daughters and mothers selling their bodies for fifty cents. For two dollars a man could stay all night. Just about everybody just wanted a decent job. Work, with wages enough to fill the belly and a bed at night. I didn't take a gun and start robbing and maybe kill. My dream was to learn to read and write after I got enough money to hire a teacher. That's where I was at in 1931 when I was arrested.

CHAPTER FOUR

Death Row

It was early afternoon in late April when they came to take eight of us to Kilby Prison; Roy Wright was left behind in the Jefferson County Jail. We were carried off in four private cars, two of us handcuffed in the back seats and a guard in the back and front, plus the driver. It was a pretty spring day, the drive took some hours, and I almost had a sense of being free for a while. Kilby Prison was on the outskirts of Montgomery in the middle of nothing. All of a sudden I saw the big, gray concrete walls with the barbed wire stretched along the top. There was little tower buildings on the corners and midway the walls. Men were in these towers with rifles and machine guns. Here I was to spend most of the next fifteen years of my life.

We went through several steel gates until we got to a two-story building. The guards took us to the second floor into a bathroom. They told us to take off our clothes and if we wanted to have them sent home we could.

The clothes we had weren't worth a dime. They were in rags. We'd been wearing them all the weeks since our arrest without a bath. We were as lousy as could be. Haywood Patterson was the only one to send his things home. We took our baths and we were given prison uniforms to wear. Then we were taken down the hall to the death cells.

There was a room about forty feet wide and twenty-five feet long. There were sixteen cells, eight on each side of a narrow hallway. At the end of the hall was a green door and behind it was the electric chair. There was a full house, with two and three men to a cell, all black. The death house was Jim-Crowed, like everything in the South at that time. They wouldn't put a white man in a cell with a black man. They kept them in a little place outside, with white prisoners who had committed misdemeanor crimes. They stayed there until Alabama had killed enough black men to give a white man a cell to himself.

I was put into a cage with Olen Montgomery. This was good because he could read and write for me and he didn't mind doing it. The cell had two double-decker-bunks, a face bowl and a commode. It wasn't big enough to take five steps to the door. I could stand in the middle and touch the sides with my arms outstretched.

The warden came around to tell us the rules. He said we'd get three meals a day. We would be allowed out of our cells only for a twice-weekly bath. His name was George P. Walls.

There wasn't nothing to do but stare at the walls and think about dying. We invented a game with match stems and Prince Albert tobacco cans. We flattened the cans and rubbed them on the floor until they were slick

as glass. We made strings out of the ravels from our
bedsheets. We punched a hole in the cans and tied a long
string to them. Then we threw a match stem out into
the middle of the hall and bet on who could drag the
stem in first. There was an opening at the bottom of our
cell doors big enough to push our meal trays through,
and we'd throw out the can, holding onto the string,
from that opening. We played this game all day long and
through the night. They never shut off the lights on
death row. It was hard to sleep, I mostly just dozed.

We did a lot of singing and harmonizing of hymns.
Also we passed the time reading and answering letters.
The mail just kept coming. People sent us money, candy
and cigarettes. We had so many cigarettes we gave them
away to the other prisoners, gambled with them or sold
them because they got stale on us.

I got letters from a woman in England for years. I'm
sorry I don't remember her name. She sent me English
money and for a long time I didn't know what it was.
Each of us got a check from the Communists for eight
dollars a month and three dollars from the NAACP.

The guards hated us because of all the attention we
got from the outside world. They came into our cells and
abused us at will. When I think of how those crackers
did me, I wonder how did I make it. They made us
parade buck naked from our cells to the bath twice a
week. We were taken two at a time. As soon as we got
into our baths they started rushing us, and if we didn't
get out right away, they'd be in there on us with their
sticks. This was special treatment just for us.

I had a toothache, and I told a guard about it. Instead
of being taken to the dentist, he came into my cell and
sat me up in a chair where everybody could look. I told

him which tooth was hurting me, but he pulled another one. The guards held me down and the dentist gave me fits when he pulled that tooth. My mouth hurt for the longest after that. Later on they came and took me to the dentist and he shot me with Novocaine and pulled the right tooth.

One guard was a crippled cracker who weighed near three hundred pounds. He walked with a limp. I used to dream of killing him. The night I got my first stay of execution he and another guard came to my cell in the dead of night. They called me to the door. When I got there it was like lightning had struck me. I was hit in the head with a pair of brass knuckles. While I was down they worked on my body. They kicked me in the balls, chest, ribs, head and everywhere. They damn near killed me. They did the same to Haywood Patterson. I sent for the warden to complain about that kind of treatment but I might as well have been talking to the wall.

The food was grits, beans, greens and no meat to be seen. It tasted awful and smelled worse. I was scared to eat that mess, so I bought from the commissary. I survived on candies, cookies, crackers and Coca-Cola. I got fat and bloated from junk food and no exercise. My skin got grayish. I had stomach trouble all the time.

The first man I saw go to the chair was Will Stokes. He went the night we were supposed to go, July 10, 1931. They had him for killing a white man. He was from Birmingham. It was near midnight when they took him out of his cell. He went around and shook hands with all the prisoners and wished them luck. He walked through the green door and they killed him. I couldn't see into the room where they had the electric chair, but I could hear every word and sound just like I was in there with

them. The warden always asked a man if he had anything to say. Most said, "You are killing an innocent
man." Some didn't say anything. Will Stokes didn't say a
word. They turned the juice on him twice and it was all
over. No one came to get his body—few bodies were ever
claimed. The prison cemetery was called Pissy Ann Hill.

I was sick in mind and body after Will Stokes was
killed. I didn't sleep or eat for days. I had seen what it
was all about and I couldn't get it out of my mind. I saw
so many go through that green door. Will Stokes, Percy
Irvin, Isaac Mims, Charlie Williams, Richard Ashe,
Willie Johnson, Charlie Jones, Blake Ruff, Bennie Foster, John Thompson, Harry White, Ernest Waller, Solomon Roper, Thomas Burns and Jimmy Brown; all
these men were black except Burns.

I was under a death sentence for seven years. I had so
many dates to die, I can't remember them all. Living
that way, waiting, wondering and hoping is hell. Finally
I stopped thinking about whether I would die or not.
And I had to get used to other men being killed right on
schedule, practically under my nose. Believe me, man
can get used to anything. Lots of the men in the death
house went nuts, some worried until they wasted away
and died in the hospital. Some killed themselves. I
couldn't go like that if I ever wanted to see freedom
again.

Two men I really hated on the row were Richard Ashe
and Percy Irvin. In order to save their lives they made
reports to the warden about everything that was said
and done by the other inmates. The day Richard Ashe
went to the electric chair he asked if he could get a Coke
on me. I told him he couldn't get nothing from me. I told
him he was going to the right place. He said if there was

such a thing as coming back, he'd be back to haunt me. I told him where he was going there wasn't no coming back. This man had been living with a woman and she baked him a cake. He claimed he saw the woman's menstruation in the cake and that's why he killed her.

Charlie Williams and Richard Ashe were killed the same night. I don't remember Charlie Williams' story, he was quiet and didn't bother anyone.

Percy Irvin was another one I had no sympathy for when he went to the electric chair. Percy Irvin, Isaac Mims and Robert Strickland were charged with robbing and murdering a white man, then throwing his body off a freight train. Percy claimed he was an innocent bystander when Strickland and Mims killed the man. He said they beat him up and made him get off the train with them. They also made him help them steal a truck. This is what Percy told the law when they were captured. He became a state's witness against Mims and Strickland. But he wound up being tried for murder and robbery too.

Robert Strickland's sister was a schoolteacher, and she was able to help her brother with money and she hired him a lawyer. He got a life sentence. Percy Irvin and Isaac Mims didn't have anybody to do nothing for them and they were sentenced to death. The guards knew Isaac hated Percy and they put them in the same cell the night they were to be executed. They sang a song together, "Shine On Me." Isaac said to Percy, "Let's get down on our knees and pray." When Percy knelt down Isaac pulled a piece of pipe out of his shirt and busted Percy's head wide open. We yelled for the guards. They pulled Percy out of the cell and propped him up in the hall. Every time he took a breath, blood would bubble up out of his skull. An orderly came from the hospital to bandage his head. They left him sitting in the hall. That's where he was when they picked him up, carried him through the green door and killed him.

Isaac's mother came to see him that night. It was the first time she had been there. The warden said, "Isaac, here is your mother." He didn't say anything to her for a long time but finally they talked. Shortly after this the warden walked up and told Isaac to kiss his mother good-bye because she had to leave. It was time for him to go to the chair. Mrs. Mims started screaming to wake the dead. She had to be carried out. We could hear her screaming all the way to the gates. By the time she got there Isaac Mims was dead.

There was an old nigger that came to the death cells almost every day. He was a preacher, the black prisoners' chaplain. He always came in talking about "you boys better make your peace with God." I hated that bastard. He'd run around to the cells trying to make us confess so he could go back and tell the governor. He'd be in the death room whenever they killed somebody. He sang the same song every time they pulled the switch, "Swing Low, Sweet Chariot, Coming for to Carry Me Home." I think he had one of the filthiest jobs a man could have. He knew what the South was and what those crackers were doing to us. Some of the men he saw killed, he knew had to be innocent. I wondered how he could sleep in peace.

February 9, 1934—I can never forget the date. The chaplain sang his song five times. That was the night they killed Bennie Foster, John Thompson, Harry White, Ernest Waller and Solomon Roper. Mass murder was all it was. These guys were charged with different crimes and hadn't known one another outside the walls. They just happened to be sentenced to die on the same day. It was to have been seven, but one had his sentence commuted to life in prison and the other took sick and died in the hospital. I lived with these men on the row for almost three years. They killed them one behind the other. I had nightmares for many nights after they went.

Another boy I remember was Blake Ruff. He was twenty years old. He wanted to commit suicide the night he had to go. His cell was directly across from mine. He had something sharp over there. He made several attempts to stab himself in the heart. He asked me what he should do. I said, "Blake, I can't tell you nothing." He cut the veins open in his arms. The guards were scared to go in there and I guess they didn't want to shoot him, seeing as how he was to be executed anyway. They put gas in his cell and knocked him out. The orderly came and bandaged him up. They gave him a bath and put clean clothes on him. The governor himself came to the death house. He said, "What you raising so much hell about, Blake? You can't make nobody do nothing for you." Blake didn't say anything. The governor left. A few hours later Blake was executed.

Blake Ruff was a country boy out of Clay County, Alabama. He had been courting a girl and her parents agreed to their marriage. The Sunday they were to marry he went to her house and her mother told Blake they had changed their minds. Blake was arguing with the mother when the father ran in with his shotgun. Blake pulled out a pistol and shot the father dead. The girl's brother ran out of the other room with a knife and Blake killed him too. Then he turned to his sweetheart and did away with her. The mother had run off, so Blake sat down to wait for the law. Another brother came around the side of the house and tried to sneak up on Blake with a butcher knife. Blake took the brother's life. He killed four people in the space of thirty minutes or less.

Sooner or later men in the death cages will tell their story. Some tell it over and over again. Harry White was one. He was a settled-age man in his forties. He was a fortune teller from Cincinnati. He had a nice automobile and he rode around the South telling folks' fortunes. This particular time he was staying with a woman in Huntsville. One day a white woman who was a friend to the woman he was staying with came for a visit. She wanted Harry to tell her fortune. He did, and the woman paid him with money she took from her brother's store. When the brother missed the money he got mad. Then this white woman told him what she'd done with the money. He stormed over to Harry's place and wanted his money back. Harry didn't give it to him.

That night the sheriff, the brother and some other men came for Harry. They accused him of raping the white woman and stealing the money. They beat up Harry and his woman. The sheriff arrested Harry. The state of Alabama executed Harry White, February 9, 1934.

Time in Kilby was one gray day after another. I dreamed of freedom. And what I would do with freedom if I ever experienced it again. I knew I was there because I was a "nigger." An animal to be locked up as in a zoo. Except the zoo animals are treated much better than the black men in Kilby Prison. I thought I was a goner and it was only a matter of time.

I hadn't seen any of my people since I had been locked

up. I wrote my mother and told her not to put herself out trying to see me. She was in Georgia and I knew it was hard for her.

I was shocked beyond words to see my mother visit me in the death house. She came with my two baby sisters. The Communists saw to her getting there. Tears were falling everywhere. My mother told me to pray and the organizations would get me out.

CHAPTER FIVE

NAACP vs. ILD

The National Association for the Advancement of Colored People [NAACP] had several branch offices in Alabama at the time of our arrest. All over the state and beyond, the newspapers were raving about the nine black fiends who had ravished those sweet white blossoms of Southern womanhood, Victoria Price and Ruby Bates.

The Interdenominational Ministers Alliance in Chattanooga had hired that piss-poor white lawyer to defend us, but I know their hearts were in the right place. They tried to help us as best they could. They wrote to Walter White, executive secretary of the NAACP in New York City. They asked him to give a helping hand. But he never came anywhere near us until we were in the death house. By this time the case was international news. A lot of people wanted to know why the NAACP was not involved.

We had accepted Joseph R. Brodsky and Allan Taub of the International Labor Defense as our lawyers. They promised to appeal the case to the United States Supreme Court if necessary. A big hue and cry was raised because the ILD was a Communist organization. They publicized the case through their newspaper, *The Daily Worker.* They held rallies, marched and raised money on our behalf. Before we got to the death house they had Haywood Patterson's mother speaking to crowds in Harlem. Letters, telegrams and petitions poured into President Herbert Hoover and the governor of Alabama demanding our freedom. One of the NAACP's leading spokesmen, William Pickens, was angry because his organization hadn't gotten behind us. He wrote a letter to the ILD praising them for their efforts in helping us. *The Daily Worker* published his letter and it hurt the NAACP's standing in the black community.

Walter White came to see us in May 1931. Mr. White was a black man who could pass for white. He had straight hair and blue eyes. He told us we were doomed if we let the ILD lawyers defend us. He said the prejudice against Communism and blacks combined guaranteed us going to the electric chair. He wanted us to give the NAACP control of the case and said they would save our lives. He had a paper with him he wanted us to sign. He said if we signed with the NAACP, Clarence Darrow would be our lawyer.

I didn't know nothing about the ILD or the NAACP. I wanted all the help I could get from anybody. Me, Ozie Powell, Willie Roberson and Charlie Weems signed the paper. The rest of the boys didn't sign. The ILD and the NAACP groups kept running in and out of the death house. Some of us signed with one group, then the other. But neither group wanted to handle the case unless all of us signed with them exclusive. I never did understand why they couldn't work together since they all said they wanted to see us free.

The NAACP put out in the papers that we were too dumb and ignorant to realize we were being used by the Communists. Not too long afterwards we all signed with the ILD and decided to stick with them.

The teams of lawyers for the NAACP and the ILD met for two days in Birmingham. Clarence Darrow was one of the lawyers representing the NAACP. The purpose of the meeting was to join forces. The outcome was the organizations couldn't or wouldn't work together. They both issued press statements that the NAACP was no longer associated with the case.

On July 10, 1931, the prison officials sent eight boxes into the prison yard for our dead bodies. The headlines read, SCOTTSBORO NEGROES DIE TONIGHT. We received a telegram that evening from Joe Brodsky: we had been granted a stay of execution pending the Alabama Supreme Court's review of the case.

The ILD was a Communist organization, true enough. But it seemed they were preaching what the NAACP and all black people know to be true—all men are created equal, regardless of the circumstances. In America it is supposed to mean equal protection under the law.

The first so-called "red" I ever saw was Joseph R. Brodsky. He stood over six feet tall and weighed two hundred pounds. He spoke with the roar of a lion. In Alabama he had three strikes against him. He was Jewish, he was from New York and he was down there helping "niggers." His politics just added fuel to the fire. But he kept coming back, risking his life. He gave us encouraging talks, telling us not to worry. He helped us not to go crazy. I heard the guards tell him: "Stop coming to see these niggers"; "Don't tell these niggers nothing"; "You keep this up and we won't be able to do *anything* with the niggers in here."

"Propaganda!" I didn't know the word. But I believe the spotlight the "reds" put on Alabama saved all our lives. The ILD was working everywhere on all levels. Their national secretary, J. Louis Engdahl, carried Andy and Roy Wright's mother to Europe. They spoke to thousands of people in foreign countries. President Hoover and Governor Miller were flooded with mail from overseas. Famous folks such as Albert Einstein, Thomas Mann, Theodore Dreiser, H. G. Wells, members of the English Parliament and other governments sent them their protests.

Our mothers, Ida Norris, Viola Montgomery, Mamie Williams and Janie Patterson, traveled the United States, each in a different section with the ILD. They asked masses of people to help their sons. The people gave money, marched, wrote petitions to the governor, legislators and the president.

J. Louis Engdahl caught pneumonia while traveling in Europe with Mrs. Wright. He died of it in Russia. William L. Patterson, a black man, became the national secretary. He is a good friend today. He ran for mayor of New York City in 1932. He led a march for us to the White House, five thousand strong. He brought a group of our mothers to see us in the death house. He said the warden asked him, "What niggers did you come to see?" Mr. Patterson told him they had come to see the Scottsboro defendants. The warden told the guard, "Take these niggers up to see those Scottsboro niggers."

William Patterson is the man who went to Samuel S. Leibowitz and hired him to defend us in the new trials.

He told us Leibowitz was an able man, an able lawyer. He said he was the best criminal lawyer in the United States, a gangsters' lawyer who had never lost a case. Al Capone had been one of his clients. Leibowitz, Mr. Patterson said, was considered a master at cross-examination.

Joe Brodsky, Irving Schwab and George Chamlee fought our case before the Alabama Supreme Court. The attorney general of Alabama, Thomas G. Knight, Jr., appeared for the state. His daddy, Thomas G. Knight, Sr., was one of the judges on the court. All our convictions were upheld, except for Eugene Williams. They said he was too young to have been tried with the rest, and they turned his case over to the juvenile courts. May 13, 1932, was the new date given the remaining seven of us to die.

The ILD hired Walter Pollack, one of the greatest constitutional lawyers that ever lived, to take our case to the United States Supreme Court. Six months later on November 7, 1932, we were granted new trials based on the landmark decision in *Powell vs. Alabama*. The court said our constitutional rights were violated under the Fourteenth Amendment dealing with "due process" and the right to equal protection under the law. The decision of the lower court was reversed on the grounds we hadn't adequate counsel at Scottsboro.

We were moved from Kilby Prison to the Jefferson County Jail in Birmingham. Our second trials began March, 1933, in Decatur in Morgan County.

CHAPTER SIX

Judge Horton Presides

Samuel Leibowitz agreed to take on the case for his expenses only. He interviewed me in the death house and he said he believed we were innocent. He read the transcripts from the trials at Scottsboro and decided the state of Alabama had attempted to murder us without a shred of evidence. Since we were innocent, Victoria Price and Ruby Bates were lying. He proceeded to investigate their past lives. Leibowitz worked with Joe Brodsky, George Chamlee, Elias Schwartzbart and many others. They got depositions and affidavits from people who swore the women were prostitutes. They found Lester Carter, one of the white boys we threw off the train. He swore he and another boy had sex with Victoria and Ruby in a hobo jungle the night before our arrest. He said Orville Gilley, the white boy we let stay on the train, had told him nobody had raped those girls. It was learned Victoria Price had served time for fornication with a married man. A model of the eighty-seven-car train was made to be an exhibit in the courtroom. The preparation for the new trials was thorough and extensive. Leibowitz tried to leave no stone unturned.

His life was threatened to the point where Mayor Fiorello H. LaGuardia sent two New York City detectives to Alabama to guard him. Mrs. Leibowitz joined her husband to cook his food because the crackers threatened to poison him.

The trials were scheduled for March 1933 in Decatur. Leibowitz managed to get a change of venue. The Decatur jail was a hellhole. It was declared unfit for white prisoners over a year before we got there. But the state thought it was all right for "niggers." It was filthy, dust everywhere, big holes were in the floors and walls, plaster fell down around our heads, the stink was sickening and rats the size of rabbits had the run of the place. But the bedbugs! There were millions of them, large as grains of rice. They crawled all over us at night and sleep was hard to come by. The bloodsuckers almost drained us dry. We raised hell about these bugs and they gave us some powder to kill them. But they just ate that stuff and came back for more.

Crowds came to Decatur thicker than at Scottsboro, but they were quiet and orderly. Just the same, the National Guard was with us all the time. There was no end to the photographers and reporters.

The judge, James Edward Horton, kept order in his courtroom. Everybody had to have a seat and he didn't allow for no uproar. He made the spectators behave themselves or he had them thrown out.

Haywood Patterson was the first to be tried.

Leibowitz made a motion to Judge Horton to overturn the original 1931 indictments. He wanted them quashed on the grounds no Negroes were on the grand jury. This was a violation of our civil rights under the Fourteenth Amendment to the Constitution. Judge Horton overruled the motion. Then Leibowitz asked for the jury rolls of Morgan County to show there were no Negroes on the list, so the new trials would be unconstitutional too. He made a motion to dismiss. To support his efforts Leibowitz produced witnesses that testified they had never seen or heard of black men serving on a jury in Alabama. Victoria Price was the first witness for the state. She got on the stand and told her lies again. The doctor testified. The state produced a string of witnesses who swore they saw us raping the two women as the train went by their farms. They were standing in their fields, their haylofts, doorways, and they testified they were eyewitnesses to the rapes as the train sped by. Leibowitz wanted to know why they just went back to what they were doing instead of calling the law. Then he produced photographs to show it was physically impossible for these witnesses to have seen what they testified they saw.

The highlight of the trial was Ruby Bates' testimony. She came in at the last and testified for the defense. She said she had a change of heart; her conscience was bothering her. She swore she was not raped and neither was Victoria. Everybody in the courtroom got very excited at this. The prosecutor, Attorney General Thomas Knight, was angry. He accused Ruby Bates of having been paid off. But he didn't shake her story.

Leibowitz put on a brilliant defense. He was confident Haywood would not be convicted, although he was mad as hell about the racism the prosecution threw in every chance it got. During the prosecutor's summation he told the jury to find the defendant guilty and show the world they could not be swayed by "Jews or Jew money from New York."

The jury was out almost twenty-four hours. We thought this was a good sign. They came back into the courtroom with broad smiles and laughing. They found Haywood Patterson guilty as charged and fixed his punishment at death in the electric chair. Judge Horton gave Haywood the date June 16, 1933, to be electrocuted. The sentence was stayed on a motion by the defense for a new trial.

Charlie Weems was to be tried next. Judge Horton postponed his trial and the rest of our trials "until such time as the passions of the local citizens have subsided."

The citizens' passions were high because after the trial Leibowitz went back to New York and was interviewed by all the major news chains. He spoke at meetings and rallies in Harlem and all over the city. He didn't have nothing good to say about the "snuff-dipping, ignorant, bloodthirsty rednecks" of Morgan County, Alabama.

On June 22, 1933, the lawyers for the defense asked Judge Horton for a new trial in the case of Haywood Patterson. The judge ordered one and issued the following lengthy statement that day giving his reasons based on the grounds that the conviction was against the weight of the evidence:

> With seven boys present at the beginning of this trouble, with one seeing the entire affair, with some fifty or sixty persons meeting them at Paint Rock and taking the women, the white boy Gilley, and the nine negroes in charge, with two physicians examining the women within one to one and one half hours,

according to the tendency of all the evidence, after the occurrence of the alleged rape, and with the acts charged committed in broad daylight, we should expect from all this cloud of witnesses or from the mute but telling physical condition of the women or their clothes some one fact in corroboration of this story.

Let us consider the rich field from which such corroboration may be gleaned.

1. Seven boys on the gondola at the beginning of the fight, and Orville Gilley, the white boy, who remained on the train, and who saw the whole performance.

2. The wound inflicted on the side of Victoria Price's head by the butt-end of a pistol from which the blood did flow.

3. The lacerated and bleeding back of the body, a part of which was stripped of clothing and lay on jagged sharp rock, which body two physicians carefully examined for injuries shortly after the occurrence.

4. Semen in the vagina and its drying and starchy appearance in the pubic hair and surrounding parts.

5. Two doctors who could testify that they saw her coat all spattered over with semen; who could testify to the blood and semen on her clothes, and to the bleeding vagina.

6. Two doctors who could testify to the wretched condition of the women, their wild eyes, dilated pupils, fast breathing, and rapid pulse.

7. The semen which must have eventually appeared with increasing evidence in the pants of the rapists as each wallowed in its spreading ooze. The

prosecutrix testified semen was being emitted by her rapists, and common sense tells us six discharges is a considerable quantity.

8. Live spermatozoa, the active principle of semen, would be expected in the vagina of the female from so recent discharges.

9. The washing before the first trial by Victoria Price of the very clothes which she claimed were stained with semen and blood.

Taking up these points in order, what does the record show?

None of the seven white boys was put on the stand, except Lester Carter, and he contradicted her.

Returning to the pistol lick on the head. The doctor testifies: "I did not sew up any wound on this girl's head; I did not see any blood on her scalp. I don't remember my attention being called to any blood or blow on the scalp."

Next was she thrown and abused, as she states she was, upon the chert—the sharp, jagged rock?

Dr. Bridges states as to physical hurts—we found some small scratches on the back part of the wrist; she had some blue places in the small of the back, low down in the soft part, three or four bruises about like the joint of your thumb, small as a pecan, and then on the shoulders a blue place about the same size—and we put them on the table, and an examination showed no lacerations.

Victoria Price testified that as the negroes had repeated intercourse with her she became wetter and wetter around her private parts.

Dr. Bridges and Dr. Lynch examined her; they looked for semen around her private parts; they found on the inside of her thighs some dirty places. The dirty places were dry and infiltrated with heavy dust and dirt. The vagina is examined to see whether or not any semen was in the vagina. He takes a cotton swab and with the aid of a speculum and headlight inserts the cotton mop into the woman's vagina and swabs around the cervix, which is the mouth of the uterus or womb. He extracts the substance adhering to the cotton and places this substance under a microscope. He finds that there are spermatozoa in the vagina. He finds this spermatozoa to be non-motile. He says that non-motile means the spermatozoa were dead.

Was there any evidence of semen on the clothes of any of the negroes?

Though these negroes were arrested just after the alleged acts, and though their clothes and pants were examined or looked over by the officers, not a witness testified as to seeing any semen or even any wet or damp spots on their clothes.

What of the coat of the woman spattered with semen and the blood and semen on the clothes and the bleeding vagina?

Dr. Bridges says he did not see any blood coming from her vagina; that Mrs. Price had on step-ins, but did not state they were torn or had blood or semen on them. Not a word from this doctor of the blood and semen on the dress; not a word of the semen all spattered over the coat.

What of the physical appearance of these two women when the doctors saw them?

Dr. Bridges says when the two women were brought to his office neither was hysterical, or nervous about it at all. He noticed nothing unusual about their respiration and their pulse was normal. Such a normal physical condition is not the natural accompaniment or result of so horrible an experience.

Lastly, before leaving Dr. Bridges let us quote his summary of all that he observed:

"Q. In other words the best you can say about the whole case is that both these women showed they had had intercourse?

"A. Yes, sir."

Is there corroboration in this? We think not, especially as the evidence points strongly to Victoria Price having intercourse with one Tiller on several occasions just before leaving Huntsville. That she slept in a hobo jungle in Chattanooga, side by side with a man. The dead spermatozoa and the dry dirty spots would be expected from those earlier acts.

THE COURT'S COMMENTS ON THE STATE'S CASE

This is the State's evidence. It corroborates Victoria Price slightly, if at all, and her evidence is so contradictory to the evidence of the doctors who examined her that it has been impossible for the Court to reconcile their evidence with hers.

Next, was the evidence of Victoria Price reasonable or probable? Were the facts stated reasonable? This is one of the tests the law applies.

Rape is a crime usually committed in secrecy. A secluded place or a place where one ordinarily would not be observed is the natural selection for the scene of such a crime. The time and place and stage of this alleged act are such to make one wonder and question did such occur under such circumstances. The day is a sunshiny day the latter part in March; the time of day is shortly after the noon hour. The place is upon a gondola or car without a top. This gondola, according to the evidence of Mr. Turner, the conductor, was filled to within six inches to twelve or fourteen inches of the top with chert, and according to Victoria Price up to one and one half feet or two feet of the top. The whole performance necessarily being in plain view of any one observing the train as it passed. Open gondolas on each side.

On top of this chert twelve negroes rape two white women; they undress them as they are standing up on this chert; the prosecuting witness then is thrown down and with one negro continuously kneeling over her with a knife at her throat, one or more holding her legs, six negroes successively have intercourse with her on top of that chert; as one arises off of her person, another lies down upon her; those not engaged are standing or sitting around; this continues without intermission although that freight train travels for some forty miles through the heart of Jackson County; through Fackler, Hollywood, Scottsboro, Larkinsville, Lin Rock, and Woodsville, slowing up in several of these places until it is halted at Paint Rock; Gilley, a white boy, pulled back on the train by the negroes, and sitting off, according to Victoria Price, in one end of the gondola, a witness to the whole scene; yet he stays on the train, and he does not attempt to get off of the car at any of the places it slows up to call for help; he does not go back to the caboose to report to the conductor or to the engineer in the engine, although no compulsion is being exercised on him, and instead of there being any threat of danger to him from the negroes, they themselves have pulled him back on the train to prevent his being injured from jumping from the train after it had increased its speed; and in the end by a fortuitous circumstance just before the train pulls into Paint Rock, the rapists cease and just in the nick of time the overalls are drawn up and fastened and the women appear clothed as the posse sights them. The natural inclination of the mind is to doubt and to seek further search.

Her manner [Victoria Price's] of testifying and demeanor on the stand militate against her. Her testimony was contradictory, often evasive, and time and again she refused to answer pertinent questions. The gravity of the offense and the importance of her testimony demanded candor and sincerity. In addition to this the proof tends strongly to show that she knowingly testified falsely in many material aspects of the case. All this requires the more careful scrutiny of her evidence.

The Court has heretofore devoted itself particularly to the State's evidence; this evidence fails to corroborate Victoria Price in those physical facts; the condition of the woman raped necessarily speaking more powerfully than any witness can speak who did not view the performance itself.

COMMENT ON CREDIBILITY OF VICTORIA PRICE

The Court will next consider her credibility, and in doing so, some of the evidence offered for the defendant will also come in for consideration. In considering any evidence for the defendant which would tend to show that Victoria Price swore falsely, the Court will exclude the evidence of witnesses for the defendant, who themselves appear unworthy of credit, unless the facts and circumstances so strongly corroborate that evidence that it appears true.

Lester Carter was a witness for the defendant; he was one of the white boys ejected from the train below Stevenson. Whether or not he is entitled to entire credit is certainly a question of great doubt; but where the facts and circumstances corroborate him, and where there is a failure of the State to disprove his testimony with witnesses on hand to disprove it, the Court sees no reason to capriciously reject all he said.

Victoria Price denied she knew him until she arrived at Scottsboro. It became a question to be considered as to whether Lester Carter knew her at Huntsville and saw her committing adultery on several occasions with one Tiller just before leaving for Chattanooga, and returning on the freight the next day. The facts he testified to might easily account for the dead spermatozoa in her vagina. He says he met Victoria Price and Tiller while in jail at Huntsville; that all three were inmates at the same time; that Ruby Bates visited them (Tiller and Victoria Price) while they were in jail; that after all had gotten out, and he had finished his sentence, he stayed in the home of Tiller and his wife, and he and Tiller would go out and be with these girls; that they all planned the Chattanooga trip together, and that just before the trip, or the night before, all were engaged in adulterous intercourse.

Next Carter said that when he and Ruby Bates and Victoria Price arrived in Chattanooga about eight o'clock at night, all went to what is known as the "hoboes jungle," a place where tramps of all descriptions spent the night in the open. There are numerous witnesses who corroborate him in this statement; that they met the boy Gilley and all four slept side by side, he by the side of Ruby Bates and Victoria Price by the side of Gilley.

Victoria Price said that she and Ruby Bates went to Chattanooga seeking work; that they went alone and spent the night at Mrs. Callie Brochie's, a friend of hers formerly living in Huntsville, but who had moved to Chattanooga. Was this true? The Chattanooga directory was introduced in evidence; residents of Chattanooga, both white and colored, took the stand stating that no such woman as Callie Brochie lived in Chattanooga and had not ever lived there as far as they knew. Though Victoria Price made this statement more than two years ago at Scottsboro, no witness was offered either from Chattanooga or Huntsville showing any such woman had ever lived in either such place.

Victoria Price said the negroes jumped off a box car over their heads into the gondola, where she, Ruby Bates and the seven white boys were riding, with seven knives and two pistols and engaged in a fight with the white boys. The conductor of the train stated there were eight gondola cars together on the train; that the women were in one of the middle cars, and there were three gondola cars between the car they were riding and the nearest box-car. Lester Carter stated that he was one of the seven boys engaged in the fight with the negroes and that he did not see a single knife or pistol in the hands of the negroes. And although these seven white boys were kept in jail at Scottsboro until after the first trial no one testified to any knife or pistol wounds on any of them.

Further there was evidence of trouble between Victoria Price and the white boys in the jail at Scottsboro because one or more of them refused to go on the witness stand and testify as she did concerning the rape; that Victoria Price indicated that by doing so they would all get off lighter.

The defendant and five of the other negroes charged with participating in this crime at the same time went on the stand and denied any participation in the rape; denied that they knew anything about it, and denied that they saw any white women on the train. Four of them did state they took part in the fight with the white boys that occurred on the train. Two of them testified that they knew nothing of the fight nor of the girls, and were on an entirely different part of the train. Each one of these two testified as to physical infirmities. One testified he was so diseased he could hardly walk, and he was examined at Scottsboro according to the evidence and was found to be diseased. The other testified that one eye was entirely out and that he could only see sufficiently out of the other to walk unattended. The physical condition of this prisoner indicates apparently great defect of vision. He further testified that he was on an oil-tank car near the rear of the train, about the seventh car from the rear; that he stayed on this oil-tank all the time and that he was taken from off this oil-tank. The evidence of one of the trainmen tends to show that one of the negroes was taken off of an oil-tank toward the rear of the train.

This near-blind boy was among those whom Victoria Price testified was in the fight and in the party which raped her and Ruby Bates. The facts strongly contradict any such statement.

CONCLUSION

History, sacred and profane, and the common experience of mankind teach us that women of the character shown in this case are prone for selfish reasons to make false accusations both of rape and of insult upon the slightest provocation, or even without provocation for ulterior purposes. These women are shown, by the great weight of the evidence, on this very day before leaving Chattanooga, to have falsely accused two negroes of insulting them, and of almost precipitating a fight between one of the white boys they were in company with and these two negroes. This tendency on the part of the women shows that they are predisposed to make false accusations upon any occasion whereby their selfish ends may be gained.

The Court will not pursue the evidence any further.

As heretofore stated the law declares that a defendant should not be convicted without corroboration where the testimony of the prosecutrix bears on its face indications of improbability or unreliability and particularly when it is contradicted by other evidence.

The testimony of the prosecutrix in this case is not only uncorroborated, but it also bears on its face indications of improbability and is contradicted by other evidence, and in addition thereto the evidence greatly preponderates in favor of the defendant. It therefore becomes the duty of the Court under the law to grant the motion made in this case.

It is therefore ordered and adjudged by the Court that the motion be granted; that the verdict of the jury in this case and the judgment of the Court sentencing this defendant to death be set aside and that a new trial be and the same is hereby ordered.

JAMES E. HORTON,
Circuit Judge

The judge issued this statement from a courtroom in his hometown of Athens. The ILD lawyers, George Chamlee and Osmond K. Fraenkel, were there representing us. Attorney General Knight was present for the state. The place was packed with reporters and the local citizens. Make no doubt, the judge's decision caused quite a stir. But if he figured his decision would end our prosecution, he was wrong. The attorney general announced the state would retry us as soon as they could.

For my part, I think Judge Horton was a brave man. He lost his judgeship in the next election and disappeared from public life. He and his family must have been tormented in many ways. I can't make him out to be a complete hero though. He should have gone all the way and dismissed the charges. He had the power. He could have ended our hell in 1933. As it was I didn't get out of the penitentiary until 1946, and Haywood Patterson and Andy Wright stayed locked up for years after I was gone.

Everybody knew we were innocent, but that didn't stop them from trying to send us to the chair. The word of two white tramps was worth more than the lives of nine black men. The honor of these whores had to be upheld at all cost or Alabama would lose face before the rest of the world. Nobody was going to tell them how to handle "their niggers."

In the election that defeated Judge Horton, Attorney General Knight became the state's lieutenant governor.

CHAPTER SEVEN

Callahan's Courtroom

Haywood Patterson went on trial for the third time in November, 1933, before Judge William Washington Callahan. This judge was a redneck from the word go. His robes might as well have been those of the Ku Klux Klan. It didn't matter to him if we were innocent or guilty, he was determined to send us to the electric chair. He didn't make no bones about that. He wanted to get the trials over with as fast as he could. He said the state had "wasted enough time and money on us." He told Leibowitz he didn't want Haywood's trial to last more than three days. The reporters nicknamed him "Speedy" Callahan.

Leibowitz made a motion for a change of venue, but this was denied. His next motion was to quash the Scottsboro indictments because there were no Negroes on the jury rolls of Jackson County. Callahan had the head of the jury commission bring the jury lists into the courtroom and read the names and the race of the men thereon. Everybody was surprised when he read off the names of at least ten Negroes. Leibowitz called in a handwriting expert to examine the books. He put the expert on the witness stand, who testified the books had been tampered with and the names of the Negroes had been falsified. But Callahan denied the motion to quash the indictments, stating that it would embarrass the jury commission.

Callahan gave Mr. Leibowitz a really rough time. He just wouldn't let him put on a proper defense. The judge rushed the selection of the jury and Mr. Leibowitz wasn't allowed to question them properly. Callahan speeded Leibowitz through his examination and cross-examination of the witnesses, hollering "get on with it ... that's enough of that." Haywood was found guilty and sentenced to death.

I was up next; my trial began December 2, 1933. The jury looked like a lynch mob; a bunch of tobacco-chewing, snuff-dipping, overalled crackers in muddy shoes. I knew they would find me guilty, as everyone did. The trial was a sham. The state was just going through the motions to rob me of my life. Leibowitz was a tiger though and gave it all he had. He had a replica of the freight train built and that was the main exhibit in the courtroom. He raked Victoria Price over the coals; he kept her on the witness stand for two days. He showed those rednecks what a lawyer should be. When he got through they knew they had been in a battle.

Judge Callahan made it clear to the jury he wanted a guilty verdict. He overruled Leibowitz's every objection to the proceedings but gave Lieutenant Governor Knight a free hand. He sustained Knight's objections all the way through the trial. Despite Callahan, Leibowitz hammered away at Victoria Price until she contradicted herself again and again. Here is the transcript of part of the trial to show the attitude of the judge and Leibowitz's fighting tactics:

VICTORIA PRICE, being sworn as a witness for the State, testified as follows:

Direct Examination:

My name is Mrs. Victoria Price. I live at Huntsville, Alabama, and lived there on the 25th day of March, 1931. On the 25th of March, 1931, I was riding on a freight train that was traveling through Jackson County, Alabama, along the Southern Railway, from Stevenson, Alabama, to Paint Rock, Alabama. I was on that train when it reached Stevenson. Ruby Bates was riding with me on that train. After the train left Stevenson, Alabama, coming this way in the direction of Paint Rock, I was riding in a gondola car. Ruby Bates and several white boys were in the car with me. The car had chert in it, what I heard called chert. It lacked about a foot and a half or 2 feet of being full. I saw this defendant on that occasion, Clarence Norris. When I first saw him on that train, running between Stevenson and Paint Rock, they was coming over the box car; the defendant and some more colored men. There was twelve colored men at that time, to the best of my count and recollection.

Q. Did all of these twelve come over into that gondola car?

Mr. Leibowitz: We object to that.
Court: I'll overrule the objection.
Mr. Leibowitz: We except.

A. Yes, sir.
Q. Did you see him strike any of the white boys?

Mr. Leibowitz: We object to that. He is putting the answer in her mouth. I want to ask that the witness be instructed by the Court to answer "Yes or no."
Court: I am not going to give any such instructions as that. I will wait and see what she says. (To witness) You don't have to answer "Yes, sir," or "No, sir." Just answer the questions asked you.

A. All these twelve men jumped into the gondola over mine and Ruby Bates' head.
Q. Did you hear any of them say anything as they came into the gondola car?

Mr. Leibowitz: I am objecting to all this, your Honor, unless this defendant is the one that said it.
Court: I'll overrule the objection.
Mr. Leibowitz: Exception.

A. Yes, sir, as they came over, I did. Some one of them, I don't know which one it was, he said, "All you white sons of bitches unload."

Q. Did either of these men have any pistols, or guns that you saw?

Mr. Leibowitz: We object to that.
Court: Overruled.
Mr. Leibowitz: Exception.

A. Two of them had pistols to the best of my recollection. I wouldn't be positive that this defendant had a pistol. Some of them had knives in their hands as they got into the gondola car. I wouldn't say, but to the best of my knowledge some of them had them open. After one of them said, "All you white sons of bitches unload," the following then happened on that car, between this man or anybody else: they knocked them off and begun to run up and down the side to see that they did not get back on, i.e., the white boys they had knocked off, except Gilley. Then they commenced to attack us girls, me and Ruby Bates. They put their hands on me. After they got the white boys off, I went to the corner of the gondola to get over, and one of the crowd in the back of the car, "We are not going to hurt you," and when I started to make my jump he hit me, he hit me, and one of them pulled off my clothes, my overalls——

Mr. Leibowitz: I object to "one of them" or "somebody"; this defendant is on trial and what he did is the issue.
Court: I'll overrule the objection.
Mr. Leibowitz: Exception.

The testimony continued as follows:

They taken my overalls off and then they taken me and threw me over on the chert, and one of them held my legs, and one held a knife on me there, and then one of them raped me and Ruby Bates.

Mr. Leibowitz: We move to strike out "Ruby Bates."

Court: Overruled.

Mr. Leibowitz: Exception.

Q. Did this defendant have sexual intercourse with you? A. Yes, sir.

Mr. Leibowitz: We object to that as leading.

Court: Overruled.

Mr. Leibowitz: Exception.

A. His private part penetrated my private part.

Q. While he was having sexual intercourse with you, was anyone holding you in any way?

Mr. Leibowitz: We object to that as leading. He is putting the answer in her mouth.

Court: I'll overrule the objection.

Mr. Leibowitz: Exception.

A. One of them held a knife at my throat and one of them held my legs. I had on a pair of step-ins, three dresses, a pair of overalls, shirt, girl's coat and a girl's hat. I got off of that train at Paint Rock.

Q. Were these colored men in the car, the gondola car, where you were, when the train came to a stop?

84

Mr. Leibowitz: We object to that as leading. He is putting the answer in her mouth.
Court: Overruled.
Mr. Leibowitz: Exception.

A. They were running out of the gondola car towards the engine when the train stopped.
Q. All of them?

Mr. Leibowitz: We object to that.
Court: Overruled.
Mr. Leibowitz: Exception.

A. Yes, sir. When the train stopped I straightened up and I got up in the gondola and was looking to see what was going on, and I started over the side of the gondola to get off, and when I got to the last step I fell, and I didn't know anything else until I come to myself in Paint Rock, in a store. That store was some distance from the depot and the track.
Q. How many of them had sexual intercourse with you on that car on that occasion?

Mr. Leibowitz: We object to that.

A. Six, to the best of my recollection. Well the train stopped at Paint Rock in five or ten minutes after they had stopped having sexual intercourse. I had done put my clothes on me and got to one side. This fellow Gilley and Ruby Bates helped me. Orville Gilley is a white man. When Ruby Bates and I got into that gondola car at Stevenson no one else was in there. No one else got in there from the time the seven white boys got in, until these colored men came into the car. We was in the end of that car towards the caboose of the train when the seven white boys got into it; in the gondola, on the chert. When the white boys got in the car they climbed in and lay down on their stomachs, feet towards us, and their heads towards the engine, they were in the other end. That is about the position we were in in that car when these colored boys came into it.

Cross-Examination by Mr. Leibowitz:

A. My true name is not Mrs. Price. I am not Mrs. Price; my husband's name is not Price. My last husband's name is McClendon. His first name is Enna. I was married to Mr. McClendon in Huntsville, Alabama. I don't know how long it was before this rape that I was married to Mr. McClendon; I had been married to him over a year or two. I did not assume the name of McClendon. I never went by my husband's name. I had another husband, too. His name was Henry Presley. I married him in Fayetteville, Tennessee. I don't know exactly how long before I married my second husband I married my first husband. It was a couple of years. I wouldn't be positive. I was married by a justice. I cannot give you the date of that marriage. I did not have any other husband besides those two. I did not ever use the name of Presley, my first husband's name.

Q. Who did you start out to Chattanooga with the day before—I withdraw that—you ever been convicted of a crime?

Mr. Knight: We object to that.
Court: Sustained.
Mr. Leibowitz: I haven't finished my question.
Court: It sounded like it to me.

Q. Weren't you convicted of a crime involving moral turpitude——Look this way please, not over that way!

Court: Now, Mr. Leibowitz, don't proceed along that line any more.

Q. Were you ever convicted of a crime involving moral turpitude, under the name of Victoria Presley, in the year 1927?

Mr. Knight: I object to that.
Court: I doubt whether this witness knows what moral turpitude is; I doubt whether half the lawyers know it or not.
Mr. Leibowitz: That is on the question of credibility.
Court: Ask if she has been convicted and I can then determine whether that involves moral turpitude.

Q. What were you convicted of?

Mr. Knight: We object to that.
Court: I sustain the objection.
Mr. Leibowitz: Your Honor just told me to ask it.
Court: No, not that way—you misunderstood me.

Mr. Leibowitz: May I have an answer to my previous question?

Court: I sustained the objection to both of them.

Mr. Leibowitz: Exception.

Court: You can ask her if she has ever been convicted of a certain offense, and I can then determine whether you can ask that kind of question.

Q. Were you ever convicted of the crime of adultery?

Mr. Knight: We object to that.

Court: I sustain the objection. (To the jury) Gentlemen of the jury, when a question is asked and I sustain an objection to that question, that question and all that involves and all inferences from it, is out of the case, and not evidence in the case, and you must not consider it in arriving at your verdict.

Mr. Leibowitz: Exception.

Q. Were you ever convicted of the crime of fornication?

Mr. Knight: We object to that.

Court: Sustained.

Mr. Leibowitz: Exception.

Q. Were you ever convicted for a violation of the prohibition law?

Mr. Knight: We object to that.

Court: Sustained.

Mr. Leibowitz: Exception.

Q. Were you ever convicted of vagrancy and drunkenness?

Mr. Knight: We object to that.
Court: Sustained.
Mr. Leibowitz: Exception.

Q. Were you ever convicted of any crime under the name of Victoria Presley?

Mr. Knight: We object to that.
Court: Sustained.
Mr. Leibowitz: Exception.

The testimony then continued:
I wasn't working on March 24, 1931, neither was Ruby Bates. I did not leave my home town which is Huntsville, on March 24, 1931, with a man named Lester Carter.
[Lester Carter is brought in.]
[Clarence Norris states: Leibowitz and the lawyers working with him got depositions from people who stated they knew Victoria Price had worked as a prostitute. She had also been involved with a married man and jailed for adultery by the wife. Orville Gilley had testified in an earlier trial that he and Lester Carter had traveled from Huntsville to Chattanooga with the two women. He said they were in each other's company for several days and had sex more than once.]
I know Lester Carter when I see him. That is he. I did not see Lester Carter at the time I left Huntsville on the freight train to go to Chattanooga. He

was not, at any time, with me and Ruby Bates, on the same freight car going to Chattanooga; if he was I didn't know him. If I had ever spoken to Lester Carter before March 24, 1931, I don't remember it. I never saw him before in my life, not as I know of. I left Huntsville some time of the afternoon before the day I claim this trouble happened. I rode on to Chattanooga.

Q. You were going to Chattanooga for what purpose?

Mr. Knight: We object to that.
Court: Sustained.
Mr. Leibowitz: Exception.

A. I did get to Chattanooga. It was getting along towards dark when the train arrived in Chattanooga. When I got off the train Lester Carter was not with me.

Q. Did you meet a man named Gilley at the train?

Mr. Knight: We object to that.
Court: Sustained.
Mr. Leibowitz: Exception.

A. I know Gilley.
Q. Where was the first place you claim that you met Gilley, on the train when you were coming back—had you ever seen Gilley before that time? A. Not as I remember.
Q. Not that you know of? A. No, sir.
Q. You hadn't spoken to Gilley in Chattanooga,

had you? A. I probably had and didn't know who he was.

Q. Mrs. Price, did you speak to any person in Chattanooga, just "yes" or "no" please?

Mr. Knight: We object to that.
Court: Sustained.
Mr. Leibowitz: Exception.

Q. Did Gilley bring you some food in Chattanooga? A. Yes, sir.

Mr. Knight: We object to that.
Court: I sustain the objection. Gentlemen, she made answer to the question. That is excluded because I have held that the question is illegal.
Mr. Leibowitz: Exception.

Q. I will ask you, Mrs. Price, where you spent the night in——

Mr. Knight: I object to that.
Mr. Leibowitz: I am not going to continue this examination if I am to be interrupted.
Court: You are going on with the examination, and I am not going to allow you to be interrupted. Wait until you are certain that he is through with his question, Mr. Attorney General, before you make any objection.

Q. I am going to ask you, Mrs. Price, if you spent the night in Chattanooga in a wooded section near the railroad yards?

Court: I see that you have gone far enough with it, myself, to make that question illegal, and I sustain the objection to it.

Mr. Leibowitz: We except.

Q. I must ask just one more question, don't answer it until objection is made and ruled on by the Court. Did you, there that night, in and about the railroad yards in Chattanooga, have sexual intercourse with one Lester Carter, or one Gilley, in company with Ruby Bates?

Mr. Knight: We object to that.

Court: I sustain the objection. Mr. Leibowitz, that question was so palpably illegal that you ought not to have asked a question like that.

Mr. Leibowitz: I except to the admonition of the Court and move for a mistrial.

Court: The motion is overruled.

Mr. Leibowitz: Your Honor sustained the objection to the question?

Court: Yes, sir.

Mr. Leibowitz: Exception.

The testimony then continued:

A. To the best of my recollection, the gondola in which I was riding was right next a box car. To the best of my knowledge, I have told the story that I am telling here now a number of times, as to what happened. I have told it at least eight times in the court from the witness stand. I told it before the grand jury and four times in Scottsboro. I told it before Judge Horton last spring; I told it here the other day, and I am telling it here again to-day.

Q. Did the man by the name of Gilley give you a little box of snuff in Chattanooga?

Mr. Knight: We object to that.
Court: The objection is sustained.
Mr. Leibowitz: Exception.

A. I was sitting in this gondola, next to the box car, which was behind me. I had my back towards the box car. I was sitting with my back up against the end of the gondola and saw these colored boys jump over my head into that gondola. That was after I left Stevenson. When we boarded that train I never paid any attention whether Lester was on there close to us or not. Me and Ruby Bates did get on the train together. We were not together with Lester Carter and Orville Gilley. We had not been with Lester Carter and Gilley just before we got on the train, all four in a party together. If I was with them, I didn't know who it was. There was several standing there. Me, Gilley, Lester Carter and Ruby Bates did not all four stay together on that train to Stevenson. When the train came to Stevenson, me and Ruby Bates, Lester Carter and Orville Gilley did not leave the train together, or in one crowd. I spoke to some of them that was scattered all around on the oil tank on that train from Chattanooga to Stevenson. I spoke to some boys on the oil tank. I did not have conversation with them. I said good morning to them. At that time I didn't know Lester

93

Carter. I had seen him a time or two, but I didn't know his name.

Q. May I ask this question: Isn't it a fact that you and Lester Carter were together in the very same jail in Huntsville?

Mr. Knight: We object to that.

Mr. Leibowitz: On the question of credibility, your Honor.

Court: I sustain the objection.

Mr. Leibowitz: Exception.

A. I know a man named Jack Tiller. He is my guard, he has been my friend. He is a married man; he used to be.

It isn't a fact that after we got into the gondola car and had left Stevenson, me with Gilley, Lester Carter and Ruby Bates, that we four alone got into that gondola. It isn't a fact that while in such gondola car Orville Gilley was lying on the chert singing hobo songs while Lester Carter was blowing on the mouth organ. I did not see or hear Lester Carter blowing a mouth organ at any time on that train. I did not hear Orville Gilley recite any poetry or sing any hobo songs while riding on that train that day. I wouldn't be positive whether I had a snuff box with me. I had snuff in my mouth. I got that snuff out of a snuff box. I did not put that snuff in my mouth while riding on the train. I had put the snuff in my mouth in Chattanooga and that came out of a snuff box. I wouldn't be positive whether I had any snuff box when I got to the jail that day at Scottsboro. I

94

didn't have any snuff box in jail. It was lost. I didn't lose that snuff box on the gondola on which I was riding. That gondola where the snuff box was found, the fourth or fifth gondola, one of the middle cars here, was not where I was riding. I remained in this gondola all the morning and stayed there until I got off the train after leaving Stevenson. When these colored boys jumped into the gondola they fought in the same gondola. Ruby Bates and I stood up after the colored boys got on the gondola. We were standing up, watching the fight. After all of the twelve got in there, twelve of them started to fight with the white boys. These twelve negroes were fighting with the white boys. Every one of the twelve negroes were taking part in the fight with the white boys. Right next to us was a box car. It was something like five or ten minutes after the fighting started before the white boys were thrown from the train. I was right close to the end of this car. I had on overalls at that time and a woman's cloak. The cloak had a fur collar.

That was when I was in a position to step from the gondola car and get on this box car. I was right next to the box car; just the partition of the gondola. I stayed there until the fight was over. I stood there with Ruby Bates. It was then that I claim that I was assaulted, after five or ten minutes standing there (indicating), next to this end of the car. I was interested in watching the fight. I looked at it to see how it was going on. I didn't do anything at that time. I stood there looking at the fight. There was nothing to stop me from getting out from the gondola onto the box car. The colored boys were engaged in the fight with the white boys for five or ten minutes. I saw the white boys being put off the train. My best recollection is that they got off on one side, on the left side looking towards the engine. Well, I wouldn't say positive how many got off on that side. I counted the twelve negroes, but not as they came into the car. I did not say, 1, 2, 3, 4, 5, 6, 7, 8, 9, 10, 11, 12. I did not count them while they were fighting. There was nine in there and three got off. I saw the three get off. That was while I was being raped. They stepped over my head and got on the side of the box car. I did not see them jump to the ground. I know they got out of the gondola, then I counted nine others there. I wasn't unconscious. My mind was clear. I counted them when we got down to Paint Rock. I counted them while I was lying down, not while the raping was going on— afterwards. I counted them while lying kin'ly on my side. They wasn't all over the car; kin'ly around there pretty close to me; none behind me. Some were in front of me, some on the side of me. I wouldn't be positive how long it was before I got to Paint Rock that I counted them. The raping stopped five or ten or fifteen minutes before we got to Paint Rock. Five minutes or a little over before the train stopped. I did not count them for any particular reason that I had in mind; not so that I would know how many raped me.

After they quit raping me and Ruby, I was kin'ly lying on the side. My face was not on the chert. I was not holding my face up. Some of them were

96

large negroes that had intercourse with me; kin'ly
heavy; kin'ly rough. Before I got down on the chert,
I was hit in the head with a gun. They hit me
between my eye and top of my head; hit me along
there (indicating). I wouldn't be positive where they
hit me. It bled a little bit. It didn't make my head
swollen there. Well, it did, a little bit.

I don't know the make of any gun. I don't know
what calibre means. I don't know a .38 from a .45. I
didn't ever know anything about the calibre of any
guns at any time in my life. All I know is that he
had the barrel in his hand and hit me with the other
end. The barrel is the end the smoke comes from.

Q. Where did you find that out?

Court: I don't see any use in taking up time with
that. I would imagine that anyone with common
sense would know which was the barrel of a pistol.

Mr. Leibowitz: I want to except to the Court's
statement in reference to the cross-examination.

He hit me with the butt. I don't know which is the
butt; I reckon the handle is the butt. The handle is
the butt end I know that. I don't know which way the
pistol was when he hit me. I probably might have told
you the other day that it was the butt end of the gun;
I don't know anything about it. Whichever part he
hit me with, he hit me on the head between the
eyebrow and the top of the head, right along here
(indicating) somewhere. When he hit me, some blood
came out, a little bit. I was standing up when he hit
me. He didn't hit me; he didn't knock me down. He

hit me. They was all scuffling around me there. After the man hit me with the butt end of the pistol, which caused a wound on my head that bled a little, I don't know whether he punched me or not; I don't remember.

Q. Way back in Scottsboro you knew something about the calibres of guns, didn't you, "Yes" or No," didn't you? A. I just has been told what they called guns.

Q. You knew all about the calibres of guns in Scottsboro, didn't you? A. No, sir.

Q. Let's see; the very first trial you testified in, in Scottsboro, hardly a week or ten days after this supposed rape, do you remember testifying before Judge Hawkins? A. Yes, sir, before Judge Hawkins, I did.

Q. Do you remember being asked these questions and making these answers: "Q. That one yonder, Charley Weems? A. Yes, sir. Q. With a gun or pistol? A. A pistol, a .45."

Court: Do you remember whether you said that or not?

A. I probably did, Judge, your Honor.

Q. Now, in the Patterson case, I will ask you if you were not asked this question, and make these answers: "Q. What did you see this defendant do in that fight? A. I seen him knock a boy in the head. A. What with? A. A gun. Q. A pistol? A. A .38." Did you say that? A. I don't know whether I did or not; I don't remember.

[It is stipulated that defense counsel is reading correctly the record made by the official stenographer and that he reported the testimony correctly.]

Q. Were you not asked these questions and make these answers in the Powell, Roberson, Wright, Montgomery and Williams case: "Q. Did you see the two men who carried the guns? A. Sure. Q. They were both there? A. There was two that had guns absolutely, a .38 and a .45." Did you say that? A. I don't remember whether I did or not.

Q. If you said it, was it a fact? A. I don't know the make of a gun.

Q. You don't know a .38 from a .50? A. To the best of my judgment that is what I called them. I heard them called that. I don't know what they was.

I don't know how many men punched me in the face; I didn't count them. I don't know whether there was more than two or not. Sure, they punched me in the face; they knocked my head around. I wouldn't be positive they punched me in the face; jerked me around; they slapped me once kin'ly hard. I didn't say my nose was swollen. It did swell up a little bit. My cheeks were swollen a little bit. My lips were kin'ly cut. They was bleeding a little bit inside. I was cut inside of my lips a little. The place where I was struck my lips were bleeding; they was kin'ly busted. I don't remember about whether my cheek was also cut on the inside. My whole face was swollen up and bruised, black and blue kin'ly. I didn't examine my back after I got to the jail at Scottsboro after the trouble. As far as my remembrance goes, I didn't find any blood on my back.

Q. On the trial before Judge Horton, did you testify—page 64 of the record before Judge Horton— were you asked these questions and did you make these answers: "Q. You lay on your back there for close to an hour on that jagged rock screaming? A. Yes, sir. Q. Was your back bleeding when you got to the doctor? A. I couldn't say. Q. When you got to the jail did you find any blood on your back? A. A little bit." Do you remember saying that? A. I probably did.

Q. When you said it, it was true? A. Yes, sir; if I said it, it was the truth, but I don't remember saying it.

Q. Did you find any blood on your back? A. I have answered your question.

Q. When you got to the jail at Scottsboro and looked yourself over, did you find any blood on your back? A. I told you I might have. I don't remember. That's been nearly three years ago.

I don't know whether this kind of rock that was in the gondola was the kind you find down on the railroad track. It was small, more like sand. I didn't look at it that close as to know whether it was different shapes. It wasn't fine sand. I wouldn't try to measure it. I know it is called chert.

Q. I don't care whether it is called "chert" or "chat" or "chet," the name means nothing to me. A. I can't tell you.

Q. You can't or won't—which is it?

Court: That question is improper and you have no right to ask it. It is my business to see that the witness is fairly treated.

Mr. Leibowitz: She is fairly treated.

Court: I don't think so. I think that question was entirely improper.

Mr. Leibowitz: We respectfully except. The attitude of counsel towards the witness when asking the question was not such as to show contempt for her.

A. I said I couldn't give the jury there any idea how large that rock was that I lay there on, and I can't. I can't give you any idea whether it was as fine as sand or larger; as large as the end of my little finger, down on smaller is the best I can say, but I wouldn't be positive.

I wasn't knocked down. I was picked up and laid down kind of hard on the chert. I don't think I testified in the previous trial that I was clammed down there on that rock. By the time I was thrown down I was all sore from the manhandling and pummeling that I got. I was sore all over my body, kin'ly.

There was one negro that pushed my head down and kept it down; he pushed me down. I tried to get up. When I was trying to get up he pushed my head back down on the chert. He didn't slam my head down. He kept my head down; he had a knife at my throat. He did not keep my head down with a knife in my face. When he put his hand on my face he did it kin'ly roughly. He didn't spare me in any way, he wasn't easy with me in any way. They naturally hurt my face. My face wasn't all scratched up. It was scratched a little bit, but not much. My face was bruised all over, kin'ly. I don't know whether or not the first negro that got on top of me was the one that threw me down. I wouldn't say that the one that threw me down was the first one that raped me or not. Some negro got on top of me. These negroes were milling all over the car; they was running up and

101

down the side; some of them raped me and some of them Ruby Bates. One or two of these white boys were trying to get back on. While I was being raped some of the negroes that were not raping me were walking up the side of the car; not to keep the white boys from getting back on; just taking a walk—I saw all that, of course. While that raping was going on the negro boys were hollering out and laughing and cuttin' up, telling each other to hurry up and get through and let him get to it, and things like that.

This coat that I had on had a dark blue lining. It was dark enough so that white spots would show against it. It was a real dark blue. I don't know whether my hips were on that coat while I was being raped or not. I had step-ins on while I was being raped. They had tore them apart. They didn't tear them off my body. Portions of my step-ins were on my body. They have elastic in them. I still had them on while I was being raped. They tore them apart like I said. I had three dresses on, too, while being raped. When the first man got through having intercourse with me, that didn't wet me all over. It wet me a little bit. It wet me around my private parts, kin'ly. When the second man got through I was still more wet. When the third man got through I was still a little bit more wet. So that as each man got off me I was more and more wet.

Court: Do you know that of your own knowledge— did you notice at the time that you were, or did you pay any attention to that?
Witness: I didn't pay any attention.

Mr. Leibowitz: I most respectfully except to the Court's question.

Court: It's the Court's business to ask a question at any time during the progress of a trial that he wants to, and if you want to reserve an exception the law gives you that right. You have your exception. Go ahead.

A. When the six men finished I don't remember whether I was real wet or not. I don't say that because of the question asked me by the Judge. I don't remember. That has been nearly three years ago. I am able to identify this negro that is sitting here by his face. I wouldn't try to point all nine of them out one by one. I know that the defendant was on the gondola. I recognize him after three years. There's lots of things that have happened that will pass from your mind in three years.

When they had intercourse with me they were not so rough about it. I don't remember whether my private parts bled. You have asked me that before.

Q. You weren't quite so hazy about it on the last trial when you testified, were you? A. I was kin'ly bloody, a little bit.

Q. Did you—will you say that blood came out of your private parts onto your clothes? A. No, sir; I don't say it came out on my clothes.

Q. On page 65 of the record of the last trial, before Judge Horton last spring, were you not asked this question: "Q. Were you bleeding from your private parts? A. A little bit." Did you say that? A. I said a little bit. Just before the train got into Paint Rock, I started to adjust my clothes, and Gilley helped me to pull on my pants.

Q. Did you later meet a boy in Scottsboro, in the jail there, one of these boys that was on the freight train, and you found out that his name was Gleason? A. I don't remember his name.

Q. The boy known as "Texas"? A. Yes, sir; that is what they called him. I didn't see "Texas" at Paint Rock.

Q. Did you see one of the white boys on the train? A. I didn't look for any of the white boys beside Gilley at Paint Rock. I don't know whether I saw them or not. I can't answer the question whether Gilley was at any time thrown off that train while I was being raped. No, sir. They put him off, but he climbed back while the raping was going on. I am sure of that. He climbed back after the other boys had been thrown off. When the attack started and they got all the white boys off he came back in the gondola. When they started attacking us. The very first violence that was done to me was when they grabbed me and asked me was I going to put out, and I says, "No, sir; I don't know what that means," and he says, "You will or die," and I said, "I would rather die." I pushed them back, and when I pushed back, one of them grabbed me and hit me on the head, and pulled me down. The first that grabbed me put his hands on my legs and shoulders and held me over the gondola. I wouldn't say whether it was before or after I was hit. I don't remember whether or not any one of these negroes grabbed me by the breast when he was raping me. No one grabbed me around the waist while they was raping me. No one of them grabbed me by the private parts or manhandled me in that way. I don't know what pain is to a man. I did suffer pain. They was kinder rough. They didn't tear my insides. I don't know whether they kicked me or not. The skin was torn in several places on my body, on my throat and on my face (indicating); not on my side; also on my back. I had one spot on my leg where it was skinned a little bit. I wouldn't say about where else. I wouldn't say the skin on my stomach was torn. It was bruised; I had some blue spots. It was sore and hurt when you touch it. I don't know whether I was black on my hips or not. They were kin'ly sore afterwards. My back was sore from lying on those rocks. After the train stopped at Paint Rock, I stood up in the gondola. I sat down while it was coming along, until it stopped, and then I got up on the edge when it stopped. I was lying in Gilley's lap until it stopped, with my head in his lap. I put my head in Gilley's lap after the negroes had quit raping me. That was five or ten minutes before the train stopped. The intercourse was over then. I wasn't doing anything. Ruby was sitting down with one of the negroes with his arms around her neck. I was lying down and she was sitting down. When the train passed the station, I was standing up looking. I don't remember whether the car that I was in passed the station or not. After the train stopped, Gilley got up, and after a couple of minutes I got up from lying down. I was sitting up when the train stopped. I was lying down when it stopped, when the train stopped Gilley got out of the car, and I sat up like I am now. I did not continue to lay in the gondola after the train stopped. No sooner than the train stopped than Gilley got out, and I sat up. I don't

THE LAST OF THE SCOTTSBORO BOYS

know whether I or Gilley called out to any man along there for help, or say, "Hey," and call the attention to anyone. I don't know anything about that. They were all hollering and going on around there. When I sat up, I was not alone two minutes while Gilley was gone. Ruby was still standing there. Ruby started to climb out. I wasn't in there after the train stopped over a second. Ruby climbed down and I got out. After Ruby climbed down, I stood up by the gondola for the first time. Gilley didn't wait to help me off the gondola. I started to climb down after Ruby got down. I was still in the last car in this string of gondolas next to the box car. I am as sure of that as anything I have testified. We were in the gondola next to the box car where the raping took place. I am sure of that. I did not see Gilley standing there. When I got off I fell. I didn't see Gilley before I got off; I didn't look for him. I don't know what happened to Gilley. I fell there beside the gondola. The gondola I was on is the one I fell off. That was the last one next to the box car. It was towards the caboose. After I fell there, I don't know what happened until I got to the store. I was taken to the store and the doctor called. A man they said was a doctor examined me in the store. I have not seen that doctor since in court in any of the trials. I don't know him. He told them to rush me to Scottsboro. They sent me on to these other doctors because I was in such a bad condition. I was in a very bad condition at Paint Rock. From Paint Rock I was in Scottsboro in about an hour and a half. The doctors that examined me were Dr. Bridges and Dr. Lynch. They first examined me in the hospital room, on the side of the jail. They didn't examine me much there; they kin'ly looked us over. I still had on my coat, my cloak, with the blue lining, my overalls, the three dresses and the step-ins and the shirt. I had a shirt on that day, too, and a hat, shoes and stockings. I had on those clothes right in the jail. After Dr. Bridges looked me over in the jail, he then took me to his office. I had taken off my overalls and two of my dresses, and washed and cleaned up in the hospital room in the jail before I went to his office. I did wash my clothes in the jail, but not that day. I did not wash any of my clothes in the Scottsboro jail before the doctors made an examination of me. I don't know whether I went to the doctor's office with my coat on. I did not have on my overalls in the doctor's office. I pulled my overalls off and two of my dresses. I had on one dress, step-ins, and my stockings. When the doctor made an examination of me in his office, he told me to take my clothes off. I did that, and he looked me over on his table. At his office my face was still bruised and swollen. My nose was swollen a little bit. My lips were cut kin'ly on the inside. My cheek—the skin was kin'ly scratched a little bit in a few places. The doctor looked at my face and examined me. He had me turn around and looked at my back. He looked at my legs and stomach, looked me all over. I had washed my face in Scottsboro. Yes, sir; I washed my hair, too and combed it. I didn't wash my head before I went to the doctor's office. I had combed my hair before I went to the doctor's office. I was kin'ly nervous and excited in the doctor's office. I don't know whether I was excited or not. Ruby Bates done most of the talking at the doctor's office; I did very little talking.

I don't know whether any of the negro boys pulled Gilley back in the train; he was in the far corner. I could see him, but I wasn't paying any attention. To the best of my knowledge and remembrance, I think I did see him. I think the negroes was pulling at something. I seen Gilley in the corner. I wouldn't say to be sure that I saw him pulled back on the train. My best recollection is they pulled him back. I wouldn't say for sure that they pulled him back. The negroes pulled him back into the car, the boy named Gilley, and let him stay there on that car all the time that these negroes were raping me and Ruby Bates. He was there in the corner of the gondola.

Re-direct Examination:

These are the step-ins I had on on that occasion (indicating). After this occurrence I washed these step-ins. I washed my clothes the next day, part of them, all of them except my overalls; I wasn't able to wash them. I kept these step-ins in my possession up until the trial held in this court room last spring.

Mr. Bailey: We offer the step-ins in evidence. (No objection was offered at that time.)

Q. Examine this knife, Mrs. Price (hands knife).

Mr. Leibowitz: We are objecting to the introduction of the step-ins. I would not have objected if they had been brought in with all the dirt and stuff on them. But when she brings in something that she later washed, I am objecting to their introduction.

Court: The objection is overruled.
Mr. Leibowitz: Exception.

A. That is my knife. I had a knife in this gondola during the occurrence I have testified about. One of these negroes taken it off'n me. The next time I saw the knife was in the court room at Scottsboro. One of the law had it then. Mr. Woodall brought my knife out of the court room.
Q. Mr. Woodall brought the knife out of the court room? A. Yes, sir; they asked me if that was my knife.

Mr. Leibowitz: We object to that.
Court: Overruled.
Mr. Leibowitz: Exception.

Q. That is the time you next saw it? A. Yes, sir.

Court: About the step-ins, of course you will have to follow that up and show that they are in the same condition they were in at the time she washed them.

That garment is in the same condition now as it was when brought into court back in the spring, in this court room. They are in the same condition they were in immediately after the rape, except that I have washed them. The knife is in the same condition.

Mr. Leibowitz: We object to the knife.
Mr. Bailey: She has identified the knife and testified that one of these defendants took the knife away from her.

Court: The step-ins are in evidence, but I will exclude the knife for the present.

Re-cross Examination:
There was four hands grabbed me (indicating), this way, to tear these drawers apart. I don't know whether they scratched me in the crotch or not in ripping these things open this way. There was a few scratches to the best of my remembrance, I never paid no attention to whether I bled from the scratches when they ripped the drawers apart.

I don't know what the negroes had on. I didn't pay attention. They had clothes on. While they were having intercourse with me they had on clothes, sure they did. When I was assaulted and while I was resisting I don't know whether I scratched any of these negroes in the face. I struck at them. I hit some of them until they held me. I don't know whether I kicked some of them or not. I don't remember. I did not tear the clothes of any of them. I did not put up a fierce battle. I don't remember being asked before Judge Horton whether when Dr. Bridge and Dr. Lynch examined me they saw my coat at that time and it was all spattered over with semen. I don't remember whether I answered, "Yes, sir." I don't think I made that statement.

[Clarence Norris recalls: Victoria Price's answers to Leibowitz were mostly, "I don't know" and "I don't remember." But she told Knight she had been raped over and over on a bed of rocks, pistol-whipped, choked and beaten. A doctor examined the woman no more than ninety minutes after she was supposedly

raped and Leibowitz called this doctor to testify for
the defense. Dr. Bridges said he found no sign of
hysteria; her pulse and respiration were normal. She
had no wounds, blood, lacerations or bruises. This
man had nothing to gain by giving false testimony.
How could the jury disbelieve such a respected
member of the community? It was beyond my
understanding.]

DR. E. R. BRIDGES, sworn for defendant (out of
order), testified:

Direct Examination:
   I am a duly licensed physician, licensed to practice
under the laws of the State of Alabama. I am a
resident of Scottsboro and have been for a number of
years. I am a general medical practitioner. I treat all
kinds of medical cases that come to a medical doctor.
I examined Mrs. Victoria Price on the 25th of March,
1931, on the day some trouble is said to have
happened on a freight train. I saw her first at the jail
house in Scottsboro. It was something around 4
o'clock in the afternoon, probably a little after. I saw
her in company with some other girl, Ruby Bates. I
did not examine her there at all when I first saw
them. I just saw two women. I told them to take
them over to my office, where I could make a more
private examination. When Victoria Price came to
my office, I told her to undress herself. I removed her
clothes from her waist down. From her waist up she
had on her clothes. This was in my presence. After
she removed her clothes, I gave her a physical
examination. I don't remember seeing any cut on the

top of her head from which any blood came. I did not find any bruises on the face. I don't remember finding any puffed up lips, or swollen lips. If I had seen that, I would have noticed it. We were looking for those things.

Q. Were you instructed by the authorities of Jackson County to make the examination?

Mr. Knight: That is objected to.
Court: Sustain the objection.

I made an examination of the face. I didn't see anything. I didn't see any blood. I was examining her for the purpose of finding marks, if possible, and I made note of everything I saw. I don't remember finding any scratch on her face. I did not examine the chest of this woman on that day; I did the next day. I did examine her abdomen. There were no cuts on the chest nor any cuts on the abdomen. I examined her back. There were no cuts on the back from which blood would come; no cuts on her legs; no abrasions or skin rubbed off on the legs; no tears of the skin near the privates at all. The vagina was not torn in any way. I found a couple of scratches on the wrist of one arm, and on the forearm of the other. I knew these women were taken off a freight train. I heard that; I didn't know it. I did not find any lacerations of any kind outside the scratches on the wrist and forearm. When I examined this woman, her pulse was not fast; it was in the bounds of normal. The respiration was about normal, too. A person under excitement, as a rule, especially a woman, would show a rapid pulse and rapid breathing. If a woman

112

came into court and made believe she was fainting, threw herself over in this fashion, if she was just faking or shamming a faint, a doctor could, as a rule, find that out by feeling her pulse, but not always. They can fake it sometimes mighty well.

Q. Tell us, doctor, supposing a woman had been hit in the head with the butt end of a gun—let me put it this way, suppose that a woman came into court and testified, that is assuming a state of facts for the purpose of hypothetical question—assuming that a woman came into court and testified that she had been hit on the head with the butt end of a gun, the wound from which bled——

Mr. Knight: I object to the question.
Court: I will wait until he gets through.

Q. (Continued)—and supposing further that she states that she was seized very violently, and states further that she was struck several blows in and about different parts of the body, including the face, and supposing that she was picked up and held over the sides of a gondola car by her legs, and then pulled back around, and thrown down on some rough material known as chert, and suppose then and there one of the assailants pushed her head, that is the head, in a violent fashion, put his hand on her face roughly, and supposing further that this man that threw her down had intercourse with her, and supposing that while the intercourse was going on, he tore at her breasts, taking hold of her in and about the breasts, and suppose that six men in succession had intercourse with this woman, against her will, while

113

she was struggling and squirming, and resisting, on this rock, or chert, and suppose, doctor, that she lay on this rock or chert on her back and on her side for over an hour, screaming and struggling with these heavy men on top of her, and suppose after that, she was taken off, and suppose that she claimed that she was in a faint, for a few moments, and was taken to a nearby point to a doctor's office—what would you expect to find on her body—can you state with reasonable certainty what would be found on her body; would you not find more evidence of violence and assault than a mere couple of scratches on the wrist and forearm, or the throat?

Mr. Knight: We object to that.

Court: The objection is well taken. The question is not based on the evidence.

Mr. Leibowitz: We except.

Cross-Examination:

A. I testified at Scottsboro three years ago. Without the testimony I don't have a distinct recollection of saying that I saw bruises on her throat. In the afternoon when I examined her I examined her from the waist down. She had on her dress from the waist up. I examined her back the next morning. I found a small blue spot about like a pecan in the small of the back. She had some scratches on one wrist and forearm, several small scratches. I can't be expected to remember every detail at this time. There might be a few little ones that I overlooked, something like that. I don't remember how many cases I testified in in Scottsboro. I think in two of them. They did not bring the colored boys over to my office that day. I don't remember whether they were brought in the hospital room in the jail while I was there. I saw one of them in the court house. I don't know whether I saw the defendant in there. I don't know one of them by name.

Redirect Examination:
Q. You have been a witness in every case for the State, haven't you?

Mr. Knight: We object to that.
Court: Sustain the objection. That he has appeared as a witness is enough.
Mr. Leibowitz: We except.

Re-cross Examination:
A. I stated to Mr. Leibowitz that her pulse was about normal when I examined her in my office.
Q. Is it possible that a person who has gone through quite a strain could regain a normal pulse in a couple of hours after the strain?

Mr. Leibowitz: We object to that.
Court: Overruled.
Mr. Leibowitz: Exception.

A. In how long?
Court: The question he has asked is, is it possible in a couple of hours?
A. Yes, sir.

Q. When you examined Victoria Price on the following day, was she not in a hysterical condition on that day?

Mr. Leibowitz: We object to her condition on the following day as immaterial.
Court: Overrule the objection.
Mr. Leibowitz: Exception.

A. Yes, sir.
Q. I will ask you if it is not sometimes the case that where a woman is normal after going through great excitement, the following day she will be in a highly nervous condition?

Mr. Leibowitz: We object to that.
Court: Overruled.
Mr. Leibowitz: Exception.

A. Yes, sir. I don't remember seeing bruises on Victoria Price's throat at this time. I might have sworn that she did before. We forget in two and a half or three years. I don't remember.

Re-direct Examination:
A. I made some notes in my office at the time I examined her. I do not have them with me. I had them here the other day. The things I put down were things I found on the body, a history of it. I did not put down any cuts on the head; nor swollen nose; nor any battered or puffed-up lips; nor any skin torn on her. I don't remember putting down any injuries or wounds, but some scratches on the wrist and forearm

and a blue place on the small of the back. It is possible that she might have had a cut on her lip that we overlooked, and a little blood, and it is possible she might have had her nose mashed that we overlooked, but if there were lacerations of the skin we ought to have seen them. Cuts on the skin would not disappear in an hour and a half.

Re-cross Examination:
Dr. Lynch probably saw them more frequently than I did. He was county physician and health officer.

Mr. Leibowitz: We now offer the deposition of Ruby Bates.

Mr. Knight: I have interposed several objections to the questions propounded to Ruby Bates, and which I think will be sustained by your Honor, in view of your holdings heretofore, and I suggest that before he reads the questions, that the jury be excluded while we determine which are proper to read and which are not.

Court: Is there any objection to that?

Mr. Leibowitz: Yes, sir.

Court: Well, we will proceed in open court. Gentlemen of the jury, that same rule of law that I told you about a while ago, that when a question is objected to, when propounded to a witness here on the stand, and I sustain the objection, puts that question out of the case, and also puts out any answer that may be made thereto, so you don't let it have any lodgment in your mind; that rule of law also applies to a deposition. Whenever a question is asked and objection is made and sustained, it is just the same as if the question was never answered.

Mr. Leibowitz: There has been a severance in this case, but before the severance the deposition was taken on behalf of all the defendants, and now only one is on trial, and I'm wondering if there is going to be any objection to the deposition on that ground?

Mr. Knight: I am willing that he should introduce the deposition in this case; the State has no objection to it.

Mr. Leibowitz: I want to offer in evidence this commission to take the deposition, signed by Mr. J. H. Green, Clerk of the Court, and all of the captions thereon. I am offering in evidence the interrogatories propounded by the defendant, by his attorneys, and certified by Mr. Green, under the seal of the Court. I want to offer to read the interrogatories on behalf of the defendant; I want to read the interrogatories referring to them by number, and read the answers, also referring to them by number.

Mr. Knight: Now, the State objects to each and every question propounded to the witness Ruby Bates, and will say, at this time, I will have specific objections to each question as it is asked, and the State objects to any rebuttal interrogatories propounded, separately and severally, on the ground that the State had no opportunity to cross the witness on the rebutting interrogatories.

[Norris notes: Ruby Bates didn't return to Alabama to testify in the trials after Haywood Patterson's trial before Judge Horton when she said neither she nor Victoria Price were raped. She had been much abused by the townspeople, the press and the prosecution for telling the truth and I guess she couldn't take anymore. And it's mighty funny they didn't do anything about her perjuring herself in the first trials. That's against the law, but she finally told the truth and it didn't make any difference to the jury. Her testimony in my trial was introduced in depositions taken from her by Leibowitz and Knight. Every time Knight objected to a question put to her in the deposition by Leibowitz, Callahan wouldn't allow the answer to be read to the jury. But the record is all here for the reader.]

INTERROGATORIES OF RUBY BATES

1. What is your name? A. Ruby Bates.

2. How old are you? A. Nineteen now. I will be twenty on my birthday, March 4, 1934.

3. Do you know Victoria Price? A. Yes.

4. When and where did you first meet her? A. In a textile mill in Huntsville, Alabama, in the year 1929.

5. Do you know Lester Carter? A. Yes.

6. When and where and under what circumstances did you first meet him? (This question was objected to by the State. The Court sustained the objection and the defendant excepted.) The excluded answer was as follows: A. Well, I met him on a city chain gang in January of 1931 in Huntsville, Ala.

7. Do you know Jack Tiller? A. Yes.

8. When and where and under what circumstances did you first meet him? (This question was objected to by the State. The Court sustained the objection, and the defendant excepted.) The excluded answer

was as follows: A. I don't remember the date when I met him. I met him with Victoria Price in a cotton mill in Huntsville, Alabama.

9. Where did you reside in 1931? A. At home in Huntsville, Alabama.

10. With whom? A. With my mother and brother and sister.

11. Prior to March 24, 1931, were you in company of Victoria Price, Lester Carter and Jack Tiller or either of them, especially in said month of March? (This question was objected to by the State. The Court sustained the objection and the defendant excepted.) The excluded answer was as follows: A. Yes, I was in their company on March 23 and 24th, 1931.

12. State specifically what occurred between you and them or either of them? (This question was objected to by the State. The Court sustained the objection and the defendant excepted.) The excluded answer was as follows: A. On March 23rd, in the afternoon about 5:30, it was nearer 6 o'clock, Victoria Price, Lester Carter and Jack Tiller and myself walked up the Pulaski Pike and then we turned off at the Pulaski Pike after we had gone something like a mile or two miles. I don't know exactly how far it was that we walked up the Pike. We went off into a side road. We walked along this road until we came to a big ditch and then we saw these vines on each side of the ditch where we couldn't be seen. We got over in the vines. There were sexual intercourse between both couples, Lester Carter with myself and Jack Tiller with Victoria Price. Later in the night it began raining, so we moved from there and walked to the N. C. & St. L. Railroad, and at first we couldn't find any

empty box car and then we went to the Southern Railroad, where it crosses the N. C. & St. L. Railroad, and we couldn't find any empty box car there. We went up the N. C. & St. L. Railroad and we found a box car there on the side track. We got into this box car and later in the night there was sexual intercourse again. We also built a fire in the box car to keep warm, with paper that was in the box car.

13. What conversations, if any, did you have prior to March 24, 1931, and in the said month of March, with Victoria Price, Jack Tiller and Lester Carter with reference to a proposed trip out of the City of Huntsville, Alabama? (This question was objected to by the State. The Court sustained the objection. The defendant excepted.) The excluded answer read as follows: A. On the morning of March 24th, early in the morning about 5 o'clock, Victoria Price, Lester Carter, Jack Tiller and myself were together and it was discussed between us about leaving that day, which was on Thursday, March 24th, and we planned to meet at 11 o'clock that day on the Southern Railroad at the Athens Crossing.

14. Did Victoria Price have intercourse with Jack Tiller a day or two before March 25, 1931, in your presence and in the presence of Lester Carter? (The question was objected to by the State. The Court sustained the objection. Defendant excepted.) The excluded answer was as follows: A. On the night of March 23rd, yes.

15. What occurred on March 24, 1931, in your presence between Lester Carter, Jack Tiller and Victoria Price? (The question was objected to by the State. The Court sustained the objection. Defendant

excepted.) The excluded answer was as follows: A. I don't know what they mean. Unless this is the answer. Jack Tiller did not go with us on account of his wife. Of course, we was all talking. There was nothing done except talking and Jack Tiller said for us to go ahead and that he would join us in a few days and that he did not go on account of his wife.

Q. Did you, Lester Carter and Victoria Price board a freight train in the City of Huntsville, Alabama, and proceed on said freight train to Chattanooga, Tenn.? A. Yes.

16. State the details and circumstances concerning the said ride mentioned in the preceding paragraph. (The State objected to the question. The Court sustained the objection. The defendant excepted.) The excluded answer was as follows: A. When we first got on this freight train going to Chattanooga, we got in a box car. The box car had a lot of white men and also there was some colored men in the car—but did not speak to us for a long time. There was one boy in the car who knew myself and he came to where we was. We was in the other end of the car and he was at the other end of the car with the rest of the hobos. When he got off the train he said "Good luck" to us. The train pulled into Chattanooga that night about 8:30.

17. Upon arrival at Chattanooga, did you meet one Orville Gilley? State the circumstances of such meeting, who was present, and what was said by Victoria Price, Lester Carter and you and Orville Gilley. (The State objected to the question. The Court sustained the objection. The defendant excepted.) The excluded

answer was as follows: A. Yes. We was looking for a
box car to stay in that, because we knew no one in
Chattanooga, Tennessee, where we could stay. While
we was looking for this box car, Orville Gilley was
coming meeting us, coming in a direction to us and we
coming meeting him. Lester Carter and Victoria Price
and myself were present and Orville Gilley was by
himself. Lester Carter asked him for a match. Then
he wanted to know what we were doing and where we
was going—so we told him we was looking for a place
to stay for the night and he joined our group to try
and find a box car that was fit to stay in. Most of
them was dirty on the inside and some were almost
rotten down. When we couldn't find a box car, Orville
Gilley said that he knows a place, he knew was the
hobo jungle, a place where we could rest. We all got
arms' full of shingles from the box cars and took them
over and built a fire.

18. State in detail what occurred during your stay
in Chattanooga between you, Orville Gilley, Lester
Carter, Victoria Price and others, until the morning
of March 25, 1931. (The State objected to the
question. The Court sustained the objection. Defendant excepted.) The answer excluded was as follows:
A. On the night of March 24 after we had built a fire,
Orville Gilley and Lester Carter went to get something to eat. Of course, we couldn't see where they
went, because I don't know. When they came back,
they had something to eat and also some coffee and a
small lard bucket to make the coffee in. After we had
eaten what they got, we were sitting by the fire and
Lester Carter and myself spread out on Lester's

overcoat on the ground and laid down and we dozed off to sleep. That's all that happened that night that I remember.

19. What transpired on March 25, 1931, between the hours of 6 A.M. and 3 P.M.?

Mr. Knight: The State objects to that—some parts may be admissible, but some parts are not. I am objecting to that part of the question that calls for anything prior to boarding the train at Chattanooga on March 25th.

Court: I can't pass on it until I see the answer. (Court takes answer and reads it.)

Mr. Leibowitz: This testimony, whatever it is, is offered for the purpose of impugning the chastity of Victoria Price, not for the purpose of attacking her credibility, but to explain away the condition the girl was found in by the doctor—the question is for that purpose, and not for attacking her credibility.

Court: I'll exclude all of her answer, beginning on page 5, down to and including the word "West" on page 6.

Mr. Leibowitz: Exception.

(The excluded part of the answer is included in brackets from beginning of answer. After the brackets close, answer is admitted.) A. [On the morning of March 25th, Lester Carter and Orville Gilley went again for something to eat, and while they was gone, Victoria Price and myself got some water from a branch stream that was running near the place where we stayed that night to wash our face and hands. Before Lester Carter and Orville Gilley left for food, we moved over into another place from where we stayed that night. After we finished washing, we was sitting there and talking and two men spoke to us and said "Good morning" and asked us if there was anything they could do for us. We told them there was nothing they could do. Then they went on. Later, there were two negro men went by and they spoke to us and said "Good morning." They asked if they could bring wood to put on the fire for us. We told them we was letting the fire go out. Then they wanted to know if we were alone there. We told them we was not alone. That's all that was said between us and they left. Then Victoria Price looked over into another place where there was a bunch of hobos and she said, "If I knew that Lester and the other boy— who introduced himself to us as 'Carolina Slim' and later told us his name was Orville Gilley, would not come back soon, we would go over there and make some money from these boys." Then we went up on the railroad and we were sitting on the railroad and we saw Lester coming down the railroad, and when Lester joined us, Victoria Price told Lester that we had been insulted by a negro and it made Lester Carter mad. Lester Carter said he would kill him if he could find him. So Lester Carter hunted all over the swamp and he couldn't find anybody that had said anything to us but "Good morning." Then he went over to a bunch of negro hobos and asked them had they saw us or said anything to us. They said "No." So he cussed one of the negroes out and called him dirty names. That was what he told us when he came back to where we was. After this I got a chance to tell Lester Carter better, that there was no negroes insulted us or anyone else. Then Orville Gilley joined us. Only a few minutes after Orville Gilley joined us, we went down to the freight yards. We sat at the freight yard until the freight train pulled in going west.] When the train pulled in we caught the train. We got on this train. We got between a box car and an oil tank. We sat down on the end of this oil tank and there were two other men and I neither saw them since nor have I ever saw them before they got on the train at the same time we did and sat down with us. Then we had been going for some time when there was a bunch of hobos coming on the train and they were just walking on the train. When they passed us, they said "Hello" or something like that. They spoke to us and walked on. Then when the train pulled into Stevenson, Alabama, we got off the train. We tried to find an empty box car and failed because there was no empty box car that we could find on the train. When the train started to pull out, we got into a gondola and besides this gondola there was several other gondolas. We was all sitting on this gondola, Victoria Price, Orville Gilley and Lester Carter and myself. Shortly after the train pulled out from Stevenson, Alabama, there was some white boys come to the next car from where we was, a gondola, and they said something and Lester Carter was talking to them. I don't know what was said between them, but I noticed that there was some negroes come into this car from the top of the box car from the direction of the caboose. Then when these negro boys got to where these white boys was, there was a fight. I don't know what the fight was about, but most of these white boys got off the train. Lester Carter also got off the train. Orville Gilley started to get off. I don't know why Orville Gilley or Lester Carter wanted to get off, but Lester Carter got off. Gilley started to get off, but was pulled back in the car by one of the negro boys. After then the negro boys disappeared. I did not see them any more until there was some boys taken off the train at Paint Rock.

20. Did you arrive on a freight train at Paint Rock, Alabama, at or about 3 P.M.? State in detail what transpired at Paint Rock? A. Yes, there was some negroes taken off the train and placed under arrest and Victoria Price and myself was also placed under arrest and Orville Gilley was also put under guard by the sheriff. Victoria Price made out like she fainted. She was taken into a store, where I was also taken a few minutes later. When I was taken into the store, there was a doctor with Victoria. The doctor said there was nothing wrong; only that she had just gotten scared and that she had high blood pressure. I knew she was bothered with high blood pressure. When she began to talk, she was asked about what happened. So she told them that we were attacked by some negro boys. There was one man who told her to tell the story and there was another man who told her to shut up until she got to Scottsboro under protection of sheriffs. We was arrested by the sheriff at Paint Rock, Alabama, but those others were higher sheriffs. When we first arrived at Paint Rock, there was a big crowd there.

21. State in detail what transpired on March 25, 1931, on a trip from Paint Rock to Scottsboro, Alabama. A. There was nothing happened, only that we was taken from Paint Rock to Scottsboro in an

automobile with a few men in the car. I think it was about five or six men. I don't know exactly how many. The negro boys was also carried to Scottsboro. I saw them when they left for Scottsboro, and then I saw them again in Scottsboro.

22. State in detail what transpired during a physical examination of yourself and Victoria Price by Drs. Bridges and Lynch. (The State objected to that part of the answer to this question enclosed in brackets. The Court sustained the objection. Defendant excepted.) A. Victoria Price was examined first by these two doctors in Scottsboro, Dr. Lynch and Dr. Bridges, and then I was examined by these two doctors. The doctor only asked me if I had ever had any children and I told him "No." [He asked me when was the last time I had sexual intercourse and I said "The evening before."] That's all that was said between the doctors and myself. There again was an examination. I don't know what they did to Victoria Price. I suppose they gave her the same examination. They just gave us an examination and painted us with mercurochrome. That was all that happened. They didn't examine my whole body that day. They just examined the lower part of my body—my vagina.

23. State what transpired in the Scottsboro jail and conversations had by and between you and Victoria Price and certain white boys confined in Scottsboro jail after March 25, 1931, up until the trial of Haywood Patterson and others.

Mr. Knight: Parts of that answer may be admissible and parts might not be.

Court: Make your objections when they come to it, and I will rule.

(The parts of the answer enclosed in brackets are the parts objected to by the State and sustained by the Court. The defendant excepted to the exclusion of each part of the answer so enclosed in brackets.) A. After we returned from the doctor's office to the jail, there had been seven white boys arrested at Stevenson, Alabama, and had been transferred to Scottsboro. Lester Carter was also there at Scottsboro jail. [Victoria Price told the high sheriff, who was also the jailer, that one of these boys, who had been arrested and brought to this jail, was her half-brother.] Then she told again that she was attacked and raped by these negro boys. She told that to the sheriff. She said that there was twelve of these boys. There was not very much said about it that afternoon, because it was late and that night Victoria would not rest. I didn't know what was wrong. She was scared and we was both frightened. The next day we was examined again by the doctors and there was a few scratches on our bodies and there was a few bruised places. They were caused by the freight train riding [because anybody will get sore from riding in a freight train and staying in a hobo jungle. This boy, who Victoria claimed is her half-brother, also told that Victoria was his half-sister and kept making noise and kept trying to break out of the jail, until they put him in the same cell with Victoria Price and myself]. Then my mother appeared at the jail. First she asked the jailer why that man was in there with us two girls and

129

Victoria Price was standing there and she answered [He is my half-brother. The jailer said he wouldn't be quiet until he was moved into the cell with Victoria.] My mother tells the jailer that unless he removes that man from the cell she would see what she can do to him for having the man locked up in jail with two girls, when it was against the law. After the boy was removed, Victoria said to me that I must remember to tell the same story as she was telling me. She was at that time telling me what all she had told the sheriff. She had told the sheriff that we had been raped and she made up the story of how we had been raped, and she was telling me the story. I told her that I do not know whether I will or not, because it is not true. She was telling me that I must tell these things, as she was pointing them out to me. She said we had been raped each of us by six negro boys and that one of the negro boys was holding her feet, another held a gun and a knife at her throat and another had intercourse. She also stated that she had some money on her and that it had been taken off; also a pocket knife, that she had on her when she left home, had been taken off her from her pocket. We had men's clothes on. We had clothes underneath. We had slips and a couple of dresses. As I remember, Victoria Price had a sweater—and we had overalls over the dresses. We also had lots of visitors who came to the jail to see us. They would always ask Victoria Price what had happened and she would tell them that we had been raped by these negro boys. We were then removed on Sunday from the small cell to the large cell. There was also a cage in the middle of both cells where the men prisoners was, but there was

130

more men prisoners in the larger cell. The seven white
boys that were arrested was in this large cell. Victoria
Price would have conversations with different one of
the boys that was arrested and placed in jail for
witnesses against the negro boys. I do not know what
the conversations was about, only in one conversation
she had with one of the boys, the boy with whom she
claimed was her half-brother and with whom she had
been making love affairs since she had been in jail,
told her that he was going to tell the truth about it at
the trial and that he was not going to lie for anybody,
her or anyone else. I don't remember what he gave his
name, but I remember that Texas was his nickname. I
know his name now. Odell Gladwell, I also heard her
tell Lester Carter that he must tell that we had been
raped by these negro boys. During this whole time
that we had been in jail, there had been many negro
men brought in by the sheriffs for identification for
the other three negroes who had not been arrested,
which Victoria Price said there had been twelve.
There was only nine arrested at Paint Rock. Lester
Carter told her that he knew nothing about it,
whether or not we had been raped and that he would
not and could not say that we had been raped by
these negro boys. Victoria Price reminded me during
all this time that I must tell what she did. She said
that unless I did tell what she did, I would get her in
trouble. She would have to serve a jail sentence. [She
was then expecting to be prosecuted by my mother
for carrying me across the state line when I was under
twenty-one years of age and because my mother knew
nothing about my going away from home.] We was
also taken out into the hospital apartment of the jail,

hospital ward, to identify negro boys. Victoria Price identified a knife which she said was hers; that it had been taken off her body by one of the negro boys. Victoria Price did not have any knife when we left Huntsville, neither did she have any money. There was a lawyer by the name of Stephen Roddy, or Stevenson Roddy. He had the nine negro boys brought into the hospital where he also had us brought into the hospital where to identify the negro boys. He asked Victoria Price to take out the six boys that raped her. Victoria Price pointed out six of the boys. Then he asked me if the other three was the ones that had raped me. I was at this time frightened very badly, because there had been threats made against my life and I said "Yes." Victoria Price had also told that there was two guns that the negro boys had, I remember as being thirty-two calibre, that's what Victoria Price said. I remember as her saying there was a thirty-eight or forty-five calibre. Victoria Price and Lester Carter had a conversation. Lester Carter asked Victoria Price why she wanted to tell what she did on these boys for. Victoria Price said that she didn't give a darn for all of these niggers, let them hang them all and Lester Carter told her that she should be ashamed on herself. I don't remember whether there was anything else.

24. Did you testify on the said trials as a witness for the prosecution? A. Yes, sir.

25. Did you testify on the said trials that six negroes raped you and six negroes raped Victoria Price and one of the negroes held a knife at your throat? A. Yes, sir.

26. Was that testimony true? A. No, sir.

27. What prompted you to offer such testimony, if false? (The State objected to this interrogatory. The Court sustained the objection. Defendant excepted.) The excluded answer was as follows: A. Because Victoria Price told me these things and because I was threatened and I was scared for my life.

28. Did Haywood Patterson, Ozie Powell, Willie Roberson, Andy Wright, Olen Montgomery, Eugene Williams, Roy Wright, Charley Weems and Clarence Norris, or any of them, have intercourse with either you or Victoria Price on March 25, 1931? A. No, not any of them, with either of us, Victoria Price or myself.

29. Did Haywood Patterson, Ozie Powell, Willie Roberson, Andy Wright, Olen Montgomery, Eugene Williams, Roy Wright, Charley Weems and Clarence Norris, or any of them, assault either you or Victoria Price on March 25, 1931? A. No.

30. Up to the time you reached Paint Rock did you see Haywood Patterson, Ozie Powell, Willie Roberson, Andy Wright, Olen Montgomery, Eugene Williams, Roy Wright, Charley Weems and Clarence Norris, or either of them? A. Of course I saw some negroes in a fight with the white boys in the next car on the train, but I could not say whether any of these nine was in this fight or not.

The [prosecution's] cross-interrogatories, with answers thereto, were as follows:

1. Did you not testify in the trials of the above-named defendants held in Scottsboro, Alabama, in 1931? A. Yes.

2. Did you not then and there testify that you were

forcibly ravished by six colored boys and that Victoria Price was also forcibly ravished by six colored boys? A. Yes.

3. Did you not testify that the above-named defendants were among those who ravished you and Victoria Price? A. Yes.

4. Did you not make the following statements during the trial of Haywood Patterson, held in Scottsboro, Alabama, on or about April 7th, 1931? "My name is Ruby Bates, I am seventeen years old. I was with Victoria Price on a freight train in this county running from Chattanooga to Huntsville. I was riding on that freight train between Stevenson and Paint Rock. On that train I saw the defendant over there; I saw him there on the train. When I first saw him the train was just this side of Stevenson, and at that time he was coming over a box car with the rest of the colored boys. I could not tell you just how many colored boys I saw there; I saw more than the defendant; I saw more than one. When I first saw them I was sitting down in the gondola. There was gravel in that car; it was not plumb full. I was in the end of the car next to where the negroes jumped into it. Mrs. Price and I were together. At the time the negroes jumped over into it, there were seven white boys in there with us. After the negroes jumped in there, they told the white boys to 'unload' and hit two of them in the head with pistols, and then all of them got off but one; he stayed on there. All seven of the white boys got off but one. They had a fight with those negroes; they fought back with them. I saw two negroes with pistols, this defendant was one of them.

134

I saw him with a pistol; he was one that had a pistol, and another one had a pistol and the rest had knives, and these knives were open. I know what happened after those white boys got off the train. They threw us down in the gondola and they all ravished me. I saw some of them ravish Victoria Price. I saw the defendant. I saw him when he was having intercourse with her. When he had his hands on her. I saw other colored men around her. One of them had a knife holding it on her throat and the other was holding her legs, and that is when I saw this defendant over there (indicating), the one sitting next to Mr. Roddy (of counsel for defendant) on Victoria Price. I got off the train at Paint Rock. These colored men were on the train when we reached Paint Rock or stopped there. When the train stopped there, the colored men ran toward the engine and the people down there surrounded the train and got them off. I got off the gondola without anybody helping me off. When I got off the car, Victoria Price was unconscious at that time; she got nearly off the car and fell off and I picked her up and laid her on some grass and stayed there with her about ten minutes before the people brought a chair down there and put her in it and carried her to a store. Mrs. Price and I did not go anywhere until they brought us up here. Some doctors made an examination of Mrs. Price after she got to Scottsboro. Going into Chattanooga the day before, I saw some white boys on the train. These were white boys on the train. I did not talk with them; never said a word to them." A. I did not make the statement, but I was asked these questions. One

of the attorneys for the prosecution asked this kind of
questions and the answer that I gave them was yes,
but I did not make this statement myself.

5. Did you not make the following statements
during the trial of Clarence Norris and Charlie
Weems held in Scottsboro, Alabama, on or about
April 1, 1931: "My name is Ruby Bates. I live at
Huntsville. Along about March 25th of this year I
was in company with Victoria Price on a freight train
traveling from towards Chattanooga to Paint Rock,
Alabama. After the train left Stevenson, I saw those
negroes, those defendants sitting over there by the
side of defendant's counsel, on the train." That you
saw Weems and Norris on the train. "I say I saw
them. When I first saw them they come over the top
of the box car they had guns and they told the white
boys to unload. Then one of them hit one of the white
boys in the head with a pistol. That one on the left-
hand side was the one that hit the white boy on the
head with the pistol. Then some of the white boys
began to get off the gondola, and all of the white boys
got off but one. After the white boys got off, the
colored boys throwed us down in the car. The one on
the left side had a gun. I first saw the white boys after
we got on the oil tank. They were not the same white
boys that rode from Huntsville over to Chattanooga.
I had never seen these white boys before. The colored
boys had a knife during the fight between the white
boys and the negroes. I could not tell how many
knives the colored boys had. There were three negroes
to each girl, one for intercourse and one for holding
the knife and one for holding the pistol. While six
men had intercourse with me they stood there with a

knife and pistol on me." That you had never known or seen Lester Carter or any of the other white boys before? A. I did not make such statements, but this was also asked by the attorneys and I said, "Yes." I was asked at the first trial that I saw Weems and Norris, and I remember saying "Yes" to the attorney, but I did not see them, that I remember anything about. I cannot say whether these were the ones that were in the fight—the only colored boys I saw were in the fight. I don't think I answered such a question as to whether I had ever known or seen Lester Carter or any of the other white boys before, because I had saw Lester Carter before the Scottsboro case happened— before March 25th. The statement above was told by Victoria Price many times in jail and she reminded me just before going to trial that I must remember everything that she had told me to tell.

Mr. Knight: I move to exclude the last statement as not responsive.
Sustained. Exception by defendant.

6. Did you not make the following statements during the trial of Ozie Powell, Willie Roberson, Andy Wright and Olen Montgomery, held in Scottsboro, Alabama, on or about April 8th, 1931? "My name is Ruby Bates. I live at Huntsville. I am seventeen years old. On or about March 25th of this year I was on a freight train running between Stevenson and Paint Rock in Jackson County, Alabama. Victoria Price was with me. There was no one else with me. I saw those five negroes on the front row, these five defendants, in that car after the train

left Stevenson, Alabama. When these defendants came over the box car they told the white boys to unload. And then they attacked us girls after they got the white boys off the train. The colored boys ravished me. Every one of the colored boys I saw that day had intercourse with me or with Victoria Price." A. No, I did not make this statement, but I was asked the questions and I said, "Yes."

7. When did you leave Huntsville for Montgomery? A. On February 28, 1933.

8. Whom did you leave with? A. A girl friend of mine and two boys. The girl's name was Rosetta Brown and my boy friend's name was Jackson, and the other boy, I didn't know his name.

9. How long had you known each of them, if more than one accompanied you? A. I can't say exactly how long I knew them, but I knew them for some time. My boy friend, I knew him for a couple of years. I wasn't really friends with him, but I had known him for a couple of years. The girl friend I had known for some time. I don't remember how long I had known the girl. The other boy, I had only met him that day.

10. How long did you stay in Montgomery? A. Just long enough to have something to eat.

11. When did you leave Montgomery and who accompanied you, and where did you go? A. It was probably an hour after I arrived there on the night of February 28, 1933. Only my girl friend accompanied me. We went to Gadsden.

12. If one of the parties with whom you left Huntsville was a Mr. Jackson, state the conversation you had with him.

Mr. Leibowitz: We object to that, Judge.

Court: It appears that interrogatory No. 12 is a preliminary question to the 13th interrogatory. I'll let him read the answer.

Mr. Leibowitz: Exception.

A. I don't know what conversation you mean, because I had many conversations with him. The conversations I remember was about work. I was unemployed at that time. That's all that I can remember now.

13. Did you know then or do you know now that Mr. Jackson was or is an employee or associate of defendant's counsel? (Defendant objected to the question because it assumed that the party was an employee or associate of defendant's counsel. The court overruled the objection, and the defendant excepted.)

Court: Of course, the question does not purport to prove that he was or not in the employment of defendant's counsel, and I'm letting that in. A. I did not then and I do not know now, because I haven't seen him since I left Montgomery.

14. Did Mr. Jackson give you $20 while you were in Montgomery? A. He did.

15. Who paid for your board and upkeep during the time you were in New York prior to your appearance in Decatur in April, 1933? (Defendant objected to question. Court overruled objection. Defendant excepted.) A. I worked for my board. I paid for it myself.

16. Who paid for your transportation from New York to Decatur, Alabama, in April, 1933? (Defen-

dant objected to the question. Court overruled the objection and defendant excepted.) A. I borrowed money from the woman I was working for.

17. Where did you get the coat and hat which you wore when you testified in the trial of Haywood Patterson in April, 1933, in Decatur, Alabama? A. I bought it at Klein's for $3.98.

18. Did Dr. Harry Fosdick of New York give you a coat and a hat, or either of them, or did he give you the money with which you bought them or either of them? Court: I don't think that's got anything to do with this case; that's ruled out.

19. Did you know Miss May Jones? A. I met her in Birmingham at Rev. Clingam's studies in Birmingham the day that I arrived in Decatur.

20. Where did you meet her? A. In the studies of Dr. Clingam in Birmingham.

21. Did you make a statement to her to the effect that you came back here to testify in April because you were as much to blame as the colored boys? (Defendant objected to question. Sustained.)

22. Have you corresponded with your mother since you have been in New York? (Defendant objected to question. Sustained.)

23. Have you corresponded with your father since you have been in New York? (Defendant objected to question. Sustained.)

24. Do you know Danny Dundy? A. I don't know whether I can personally identify him or not.

25. While you were in Huntsville did a man come to see you on January 5, 1932, and get you drunk and have you write a letter to a friend of yours by the

name of Earl stating that the Scottsboro defendants were not guilty? A. I had company that day, but I was not drunk. I also wrote a letter that day, but there was no one dictated that letter to me. This man did not have me write the letter. I wrote it myself.

26. Did you not sign an affidavit before a notary public of the County of Madison, wherein you stated that when you wrote that letter mentioned in question 25 that you were drunk and did not know what you were writing and that your testimony given in Scottsboro was the truth, which affidavit was made on January 6, 1932? A. I signed that affidavit, but I didn't read this affidavit before I signed it. I signed the affidavit because I was terrorized by the Chief of Police of Madison County.

[DEFENSE] REBUTTING INTERROGATORIES

1. What did you say to Miss Mary Jones, if anything? A. If it is May Jones, I only told her that the boys were innocent.

2. State the circumstances under which you signed the affidavit referred to in cross interrogatories at question 26, in which you made certain statements concerning a letter you had written to one Earl.

A. I was terrorized by the Chief of Police of Madison County. That is why I signed this affidavit and I did not read the affidavit before I signed it.

Mr. Leibowitz: Your Honor sustained an objection to one of the interrogatories, No. 28, which asks: "What prompted you to offer such testimony, if false?" I submit that that becomes material in view of

141

the fact that she said in the Scottsboro case that she had been raped, and this explains why her testimony was given that way.

Court: Here's the trouble with your question: in Alabama the law is quite different from what it is in a number of the other States. At one time it was the only State in the Union that you couldn't ask your own witness why, or the purpose for which he did anything, and I am but following the law on the subject.

Mr. Leibowitz: We reserve an exception.

Court: I can see why you feel that it should be allowed, because most of the States permit such questions. This State doesn't, and I am bound by the decisions of the Supreme Court of Alabama, unless it involves the Fourteenth Amendment.

Mr. Leibowitz: In other words, the girl can't show why she made that statement?

Court: No, sir.

Mr. Leibowitz: May these interrogatories be marked as part of the record.

Court: The way I suggest you do that is that they show that they are filed in court, because that gives them an official standing in the court.

Mr. Leibowitz: We offer in evidence the interrogatories, questions and answers as shown in this binder, this brick colored binder, containing several different covers.

Norris continues narration:

To me the testimony of Victoria Price, Ruby Bates and the doctors is the most important. There were a lot more witnesses lying for the state. They testified they stood on their property and witnessed the rape as the train passed. Why didn't they report it? The white guy who we didn't throw off the train because it was going too fast testified that he was in the gondola and we just let him sit there and watch as the two women were raped. He said we had guns. Why weren't they introduced as evidence at the trials? They swore an oath before God and lied and lied.

Callahan screamed and shouted at Leibowitz when he did his damndest to get the truth into the record. Mr. Leibowitz was enraged and frustrated because he didn't understand that no matter what evidence he produced to the contrary, a Southern jury would never acquit a Negro of the charge of rape brought against him by a white woman. It didn't matter whether the women had been raped or not, the code of the South at that time was that the word of the lowest white person was proof enough against the most influential black citizen.

The jury was out for over twelve hours before they reached the verdict. A National Guardsman told us one juror was holding out for life imprisonment instead of death. This Guardsman had been good to us, we gave him money and he'd bring us food and drinks. He kept begging us to sing for him that evening, and we harmonized the old spirituals all night long. Our voices could be heard all over the little town. The Guardsman kept pleading for more and more songs. He went home, put a shotgun in his mouth and blew his brains out. Nobody knew exactly why.

My jury finally reached a decision, and it was death for me. Callahan wanted to put Charlie Weems on trial right away. Leibowitz was mad and discouraged. He asked for a postponement of the other trials in order to

143

take Haywood's and my case to the higher courts. The judge agreed. Haywood and me were hustled back to the death cells in Kilby Prison while the rest of the boys were returned to Birmingham.

In March of 1934 the Alabama Supreme Court heard the arguments of our case again. Leibowitz charged that the names of the Negroes in the Jackson County jury books had been forged, and in fact Negroes were not permitted to serve on Jackson County juries. He also argued that Callahan's conduct from the bench was questionable and he had prejudiced the juries against us.

The Alabama Supreme Court denied our motion for new trials on June 28, 1934, and Haywood and me were condemned to go to the chair August 31. This date was set aside pending appeal to the United States Supreme Court.

Leibowitz and the ILD had a falling out around this time. It seems the organization tried to bribe Victoria Price to tell the truth. She approached them, so they said. The ILD agreed to pay her fifteen hundred dollars. She was to meet two ILD lawyers in Nashville to give them an affidavit and get the money. But she set them up. The law met the lawyers and arrested them. They were carrying a suitcase with fifteen hundred one-dollar bills. The lawyers were held overnight and released the next morning when they posted a five-hundred-dollar bond. They forfeited the money because they didn't show up for their day in court. The state could have issued a warrant for their arrest but did not. All I know about this is what the newspapers and the grapevine said. It made us look bad. We didn't need that kind of help because Victoria Price was lying anyway.

Sam Leibowitz didn't know anything about this bribery business. He wouldn't have gone along with it. He refused to have anything more to do with the ILD. But he still wanted to defend us. The ILD wanted to defend us too and get rid of Leibowitz.

So there we were, stuck in the middle again. The people who had our lives in their hands were fighting among themselves. The press had a field day, the Southern press loved it.

We signed papers for Leibowitz that he was our lawyer and nobody else. Then we signed papers to the same effect with Joe Brodsky. We didn't know what to do. They had all helped us and we admired them both. It was a mess. Finally Haywood went with the ILD and I stood with Leibowitz. Then everybody stopped the bickering and agreed that was in our best interest. Leibowitz continued as the chief counsel and the ILD lawyers assisted.

February 15, 1935, the United States Supreme Court heard the case of *Norris v. Alabama*. The case was argued over a period of three days. Leibowitz produced the Jackson County jury rolls to show the justices the forged names of the ten Negroes. He told the court that black men were systematically excluded from the jury lists of Alabama and therefore my constitutional rights had been violated from the time of my grand jury indictment in Scottsboro.

Chief Justice Charles Evans Hughes delivered the court's opinion on April 1, 1935. He said the evidence showed that Negroes had not served on any grand or petit jury in Jackson County for more than sixty years; this evidence was uncontradicted. The names of the Negroes in the jury books were clearly forged. He established there were many qualified Negroes in the area:

property owners, school board members and many had served on federal court juries. To prevent Negroes from serving on juries deprived me of my rights under the Fourteenth Amendment, my right to equal protection under the law. The upshot of all this was that all of us had been indicted illegally. The court ordered new trials.

A few days later Governor Bibb Graves sent a letter to all the judges and lawyers in Alabama:

Holdings of the United States Supreme Court are the supreme law of the land. Whether we like the decisions or not, it is the patriotic duty of every citizen and the sworn duty of every public official to accept and uphold them in letter and spirit.

I have received the Supreme Court's decision in the Scottsboro case, holding in effect that when there is systematic exclusion of Negroes from juries, it is discrimination against race in violation of the U.S. Constitution.

This decision means that we must put the names of Negroes in jury boxes in every county in the State.

Alabama is going to observe the supreme law of America.

The Governor is the chief law enforcement officer of the State and the conservator of all our laws. All laws, of course, include the supreme laws of the land.

It is unusual for the Governor to undertake to suggest to the Judicial Department things which, under our State policy, are peculiarly within its jurisdiction. However, I have a duty to perform and an oath to abide by.

In the exercise of this power, I am writing our trial judges, enclosing a copy of that opinion, and saying that I do not assume or intimate that the contents of their jury boxes in any way fail to conform to all legal requirements, but suggesting that in the event there be any non-conformity, they speedily take propér steps to remedy any defects, and call their attention to the Jury Law of 1931.

I also made suggestions as to the disposition of any pending cases which might be affected by that opinion.

I have sent copies of this letter to all solicitors.

We had been in jail for over four years, shuttling back and forth between Decatur, Birmingham and Montgomery, from cell to cell and trial to trial. I wondered how much longer the state of Alabama would spend its money to prosecute nine innocent boys in order to send them to their deaths. I couldn't understand it then or now, the hatred. And most of the officials involved with the case tried to use it as a stepladder to success; reputations were won and lost. Organizations became larger and better known. Newspapers sold better, deputies became sheriffs, elected officials were reelected and went on to bigger and better positions. All they had to do was scream, "Kill those Scottsboro niggers."

After the last United States Supreme Court ruling, Victoria Price had to swear out a new warrant against us. Another grand jury had to convene with Negroes on the panel to reindict us. On November 13, 1935, the grand jury returned new indictments against all nine of us. There was one Negro among the fourteen jurors, he was Creed Conyers, a Paint Rock farmer. Even though

Ruby Bates had sworn in open court that she nor Victoria Price had been raped and she didn't testify before the grand jury, we were charged with raping Ruby Bates and Victoria Price.

I don't know how the black man voted, but under Alabama law only a two-thirds majority was necessary to return the indictment.

Victoria never hesitated to swear out the new warrant. I have often wondered how she slept nights.

CHAPTER EIGHT

Jefferson County Jail

Whenever our case was on appeal to the higher courts we would be transferred from the death cells at Kilby to the Jefferson County Jail in Birmingham. I spent almost three years there altogether, going back and forth. Believe it or not, I had some good times there and I caught hell too. You could get anything you wanted there except freedom. It all depended on if you had any money; if so it was a convict's paradise. You could buy women, clothes, food, liquor, whatever.

The place was run by the trusties, inmates who were trusted to do most of the things the guards should have been doing. I paid the kitchen trusties three dollars a week to bring me the food I wanted. Ham and eggs, steaks, chicken, fish, desserts, and it would be cooked just the way I liked it.

The jail housed both men and women, whites on one side, blacks on the other. The women's cages were right across from ours, so we could see them and wave to them

149

through the windows. We sent letters back and forth through the trusties, for a fee. The woman I liked was named Ernestine Dix. I sent her gifts of candy, lotion, face powder, such as that. The trusties would bring me anything from the outside world for a price. You didn't have to wear a prison uniform. I sent out for new duds: underwear, shirts, hat, pants, the works. Then I bought an iron for Ernestine, so she could do my laundry. It was just as though I had a real girlfriend. But I wanted to get much closer to her. At night the guards would open the cells for a couple of bucks and let us gamble in the hallway. One night there must have been eight hundred dollars on the table. The guard said, "Damn, you fellas got more money than me, and I work every day." I told him he could get some of my money. He said, "What do I have to do?" I said, "Take me to my girlfriend's cell for an hour or so." He said he'd have to talk it over with the guard on her side and he would let me know. The next night he said he couldn't take me to the women's cage but if I gave him her name he would bring the woman I wanted over to my cell if she wanted to come. Quite natural, all the boys wanted in on this, so he brought a few of those women over to us that night. For three dollars a girl we were able to have sex, most any night we wanted it.

Ernestine was a beautiful brown-skinned girl, she had hazel eyes and her hair grew in with tight, black curls. She had been serving twenty years for murder. A few months after we met she was released on parole. I was glad to see her get her freedom. It proved once in you could get out. I started up with another woman named Lillian. Somehow Ernestine found out about it. She came back to visit and she brought all the boys gifts but me. She cursed me out about Lillian and told me she wasn't ever coming to see me again.

Life is funny, we would laugh about it. We had the death sentence over our heads, but we were eating and dressing better than a lot of men on the outside, including our guards. Good people all over the world were making our lives a lot easier. The letters and money was still coming in from everywhere. The money made it possible for us to eat and dress better than we ever had in our lives. But I would much rather have been on the outside looking in.

In the daytime we could leave our cells and go into what we called the dayroom. We had a cell block and dayroom all to ourselves. On visiting days people would come to see the Scottsboro Boys. Lots of people would say what a shame it was to be locked up for something we never did. They couldn't touch us and could barely see us because we were behind a screen. But the warden or somebody decided to put an end to the visitors being able to see into the dayroom. They soaped up the screens.

That really ticked us off, and we decided to do something about it. On the next visiting day, we wouldn't push our breakfast trays through the opening in the bottom of our cell doors. When the guys came around to pick up the trays we refused to push them out. They went and got the kitchen sergeant. He said, "What's the matter with you niggers? You better push those trays out here." We told him to come and get them if he wanted them so bad. The warden came in with a bunch of guards. Haywood Patterson set his bunk on fire. The warden ordered the cell doors open so we could get into the dayroom. This is what we wanted, so we'd be together. We had taken the pipes loose from our sinks and we had knives bought through the trusties. We were ready to go all the way.

We stood there with our weapons, hating and hollering at the warden and guards. "Come on in, you redneck motherfuckers, come on in." We called them all kinds of dirty names. By this time we had gone a little crazy. One of the guards said, "I'll go in, I'm not afraid of no niggers." When he walked through the door Eugene Williams tried to bust his head with an iron pipe but he missed. The pipe got caught in the door and was pulled out into the hall by the guards.

The high sheriff of the county joined the group in the hall. He said, "Leave those crazy niggers alone, let them stay there and don't feed them until they throw their weapons out and go back into their cells." Late that night the guards came back with one of those big water hoses. We heard them whispering, "Do you reckon them niggers is asleep?" We were laying on the floor, wide awake. They stalked around out there in the hall for some time, but they couldn't figure out how to put the hose through the door without us grabbing the nozzle and putting it back on them. They left. They came back with a bunch of Negroes who were serving time from ninety days to six months. The guards wanted to turn them loose on us; they were supposed to subdue us. We told the guys if they came into the dayroom we'd beat them to death. Those fellas weren't about to come in there. The guards cussed them and finally took them back where they came from. The warden showed up and gave the guards a tongue-lashing: "I told you to leave these prisoners alone and not to interfere with them." He told us, "Put down your weapons, return to your cells, and I will see that you are treated as good as anybody in here, if not better." We stayed like we were for two days and two nights. Then we told the warden we were giving up. He had been coming to check us out every two or three hours. He came into the dayroom and we put our weapons on a table. He searched us and told us to go back to our cells.

That night we were served the best meal we'd ever had there. The soap was washed off the screens and we were allowed to go out on the sun porches every day. The first time we'd had the sun beaming on us in years.

I met a young man named Jimmie Brown in the Jefferson County Jail. It was between trials, and I was in solitary confinement. His cell was next to mine. He was a good writer. He read my mail to me and answered it too.

He was being held for raping a white woman. So right away we had a lot in common. I believe he was innocent too. He was arrested one morning in a railroad yard, for trespassing. The police searched him and found a gun in his pocket. That night he was put in a lineup. The woman was asked if she could identify any of the men as her rapist. She said no. They put him in a lineup six times. The last time the woman was taken off to the side by the detectives, who talked to her. When she came back to the lineup, she identified Jimmie Brown. The man was framed. I talked to him many days and I know he couldn't have committed such a dirty crime.

He was twenty years old and had only been married a month. His wife was sixteen years old. He had a trial and was sentenced to death. He went to the death cells at

Kilby. I was serving a life sentence, my death penalty had been commuted, the night he went to the electric chair. It was November 25, 1938. A guard came to my cell and said, "You are wanted in the death house." I damn near shit in my pants as the guards walked me over there. They didn't have the decency to tell me what was up. They liked watching me squirm.

Jimmie Brown's last request was to see me and talk to me before he died. We talked for some length of time. He said he had made his peace with God and he was ready to go, even though he was an innocent man. He took my hands and held them. He told me I would be free some-day. All I could do was shed tears and walk away. It was one of the saddest days of my life.

The night Jimmie went to the chair, a white man went before he did. His name was Connie Vaughn. He killed his sweetheart and got a friend to help him get rid of the body. They rolled her up in hay wire and threw her in a lake. The fella that helped Vaughn told me what happened. He got life for his part. This was the first time I had seen a white man go to the chair. After the years I had lived on death row, I never expected to see a white man go. His mother and his preacher were there. I never heard such crying and pleading. He really carried on! But they took him through the green door and killed him all the same.

I met lots of men in jail who were being framed out of their lives on rape charges. One young man named Donald Baker had been meeting a white woman and having sex with her for over a year. One fine day they were seen. The woman hollered rape. David went to trial and was given the death penalty.

A lot of people in the little town where they lived

must have known about the relationship. White people went to the governor and told him how long Baker and the woman had been carrying on. They said the woman was willing. His sentence was commuted to life in prison. Life—because he made love to a woman who wanted it probably, more than he did. He was scared the whole time he was screwing the bitch. He told me she had threatened to accuse him of rape if he did not have sex with her. But the state of Alabama would never admit a white woman was lying in a case such as this. The black man must be punished regardless of the circumstances.

John Round, Jr., was in and out of court for years. A white couple accused him of breaking into their house and forcing the husband to get under the bed and stay there until John finished raping the man's wife. I know the case wasn't that cut-and-dry because he had several trials. He received two death sentences and ended up with life in prison.

Willie Peterson was completely railroaded into prison. I really felt sorry for him. A white woman claimed she was riding along in her automobile with two girlfriends. A big, black man with kinky hair and gold teeth jumped on the running board. He forced her to drive into the woods, where he killed her two friends and raped her. I believe anyone who would do this crime wouldn't have let this woman live to tell the story.

She accused one man of the crime whose white boss said the man couldn't have done it because he was at work at the time. He was released. Then she pinned these murders and rape on Willie Peterson. A light-brown-skinned Negro with straight hair. He didn't have gold teeth either.

He had a mistrial when he went to court. While he

155

waited for a new trial, the sister of one of the dead women went to visit him in jail. She shot him three times in the stomach. Somehow Willie lived. When he recovered he was tried again and received a lifetime in the penitentiary. He died of tuberculosis in the TB prison camp.

Haywood Patterson and me were usually separated from the rest of the boys and kept together in solitary confinement. I don't know the reasons behind this. We had cells right next to each other in cell block L. This place was supposed to be for white male prisoners. But when the authorities wanted to torment a black inmate they would lock him up in L.

There was no hot water. I wish I had a dollar for every bath I took in cold water. We got no exercise. The only time I was allowed out of my cell was when they changed the linen on our bunks and to take that cold bath once a week.

Patterson and me never really got along. I had good relations with all the other boys though. But here we were locked up in solitary, side by side. Haywood was the type of guy that always kept a lot of bullshit going. We all would get dragged into it since we were in the case together. There is only so much you can do if you have your head in the mouth of a lion. He did a lot of things against himself, and that's why he was the last of us to get out of the penitentiary. No doubt if he hadn't escaped he would still be there.

There were no screens covering the bars, so we could reach out and gamble with each other. We played cards all day long. We had a big falling out behind this. Haywood won sixty or seventy dollars off me one day and I was broke. I asked him to loan me fifteen dollars for a couple of days. He said no. A few days later we were gambling again and I broke him. He asked me to loan him twenty dollars. I did him just like he did me. I told him I wouldn't loan him a damn thing. He started playing the dozens [talking about each other's relatives in a nasty way] and I beat him at that too. He went into one of his rages. He told me the next time they came to change the sheets and let us out of our cells, he was going to kill me.

The day the cells were opened, I was ready for him. I had an ice pick-type weapon made out of a piece of wire. I was watching Haywood out of the corners of my eyes. He made a move to hit me, and I stabbed him with the pick. It went all the way in the first time. The second time it hit a bone and bent. I was trying to finish him off. Haywood grabbed ahold to me and held on for dear life. The guard and a trusty pulled us apart. They took him to the hospital. When he came back he had to go to the doctor every day. We weren't allowed out of our cells together anymore. We didn't speak a word to each other for over a year.

A white woman from New York City, she was Jewish, visited us and wrote to us all the time. Christmas she sent a package in Haywood's name and told him to share it with me. He told me what was in the box. I didn't want any of the food because I thought it might be poisoned. She had sent two cartons of cigarettes, and he handed me one. That's all we said for another month.

I had a pair of clippers that I used to cut all our hair when we were together. One day Haywood asked me if I would cut his hair if he got the warden's permission. I said I would do it. The warden let us go into the day-room. I was looking for Haywood to try something, but he didn't. I cut his hair. We were up on the eighth floor. There were windows in the dayroom. We looked out the windows down at a big department store. We could see the free people walking along the street and going in and out of the store. We stayed there for two hours until the guard took us back to our cells. We started talking to each other again, from that day, and we never had any more arguments.

I was transferred to cell block P. It was the section of the jail where they brought the crazy people in off the streets. There were always five or six crazy folks locked up there all the time. They stayed there for up to three weeks until a truck came to take them to the insane asylum. I was kept in this section for ten months. They must have thought I would be run nuts. The crazy people screamed and hollered all day long. They really got going at night. When people have blown their tops, it is awful what comes out of their mouths. There were bloodcurdling screams and sounds of all kinds. Filthy words echoing back and forth all the time.

Most of the men had gone crazy on account of their wives or sweethearts. They talked to these women just like they were in the cell with them. Accusing them of fucking other men and all kinds of things. When I got sick of it, I would holler at them to shut up and I called them out of their names. They didn't pay me no mind. I had to make myself content and try to live under those conditions. I wanted to come out of there a sane man.

I remember one skinny brown-skinned guy. When his food was brought to him, he would throw it out. He shit

he Alabama National Guard was called out to protect the jail at Scottsboro, abama, where the nine Scottsboro Boys were confined. Threats of attempt- d lynchings were calmed by the troops. The Scottsboro Boys are, left to right: larence Norris, Olen Montgomery, Andy Wright, Willie Roberson, Eugene illiams, Roy Wright, Charlie Weems, Ozie Powell and Haywood Patterson. arch 30, 1931. (UPI)

'Left to right: Ozie Powell, Charlie Weems, Clarence Norris and Andy Wright i Birmingham Jail in 1935. (Birmingham *News*)

Attorney General Thomas G. Knight, Jr. reading an affidavit at the hearing on appeals for a retrial of the defendants in the Scottsboro Case. November 23, 1933. (UPI)

rs. Victoria Price photographed a few minutes before going on the stand at De-
tur, Alabama, at the trial of Haywood Patterson. With her is Jack Tiller, also a
itness in the case. November 28, 1933. (Wide World Photo)

Mothers of the Scottsboro Boys went to the White House on Mother's Day to ask for Presidential intervention. Four of them are pictured with Ruby Bates, one of the women alleged to have been attacked by the youths, and Richard B. Moore, member of the executive committee of the International Labor Defense. Left to right: Ida Norris, Janie Patterson, Ruby Bates, Mamie Williams, Viola Montgomery and Richard B. Moore. May, 1934. (Wide World Photo)

With Judge James Edward Horton listening to his testimony, Dr. R. R. Bridges testifies in the Decatur, Alabama, courthouse at the first of the retrials of eight of the nine Scottsboro Boys previously condemned to death. April 3, 1933. (Wide World Photo)

The grand jury that reindicted the defendants in 1935. Creed Conyers, the first black man to serve on an Alabama jury since Reconstruction, stands in the upper left corner. (Birmingham *News*)

Samuel Leibowitz, New York attorney who fought a four-year court battle to save the Scottsboro Boys from the death penalty, passes cigarettes to four of the freed prisoners in his New York office following their arrival from Decatur, Alabama, scene of the trial. Left to right: Willie Roberson, Eugene Williams, Samuel Leibowitz, Roy Wright and Olen Montgomery. July 26, 1937. (Wide World Photo)

After fifteen years in prison (six years of litigation and nine years of a life sentence), on receiving his parole Clarence Norris walks through the main cell gate of Kilby Prison in Montgomery, Alabama. September 29, 1946. (Wide World Photo)

Clarence Norris receives his pardon in Montgomery, Alabama, forty-five years after his arrest. Left to right: Mrs. Sara Cousins Sellers, member of the Alabama Board of Pardons and Paroles; Norman F. Ussery, chairman of the board; Roy Wilkins, executive director of the NAACP; Donald Watkins, attorney for Norris; Fred Gray, Alabama attorney; and Norris. November 29, 1976. (Denton Watson, NAACP)

Clarence Norris with Donald Watkins, his Alabama attorney, after meeting with Governor George Wallace in the Alabama Capitol building (in background). December 1, 1976. (Tom Johnson, the New York *Times*)

Left to right: Roy Wilkins, Clarence Norris and Nathaniel Jones at a news conference in Montgomery, Alabama. November 29, 1976. (Denton Watson, NAACP)

in his plate and ate his shit. One day he was lying on the floor of his cell, dead as a doornail. He hadn't eaten nothing but his shit the whole time he was there. The guards knew and everybody else, but they just let the fellow die. The things that I saw, I never thought I would see and be able to live through it.

CHAPTER NINE

A Fifty-Fifty Chance

January 6, 1936, seven of us were taken back to Decatur to be arraigned for trial. We all pleaded not guilty. I was sick to see we would be tried before Judge Callahan again. The lawyers tried to get a change of venue, but it was denied by Callahan. We were held in the Decatur jail, it was three years older, moldier, filthier and not fit for dogs. Roy Wright and Eugene Williams were there as witnesses but not to be tried as they had been classified as juveniles.

Haywood Patterson went on trial for the fourth time, January 20. There were black men among the veniremen, and that was something to see. The newspapers said it was history in the making. Most of them gave reasons why they couldn't serve on the jury and were excused. The others left after being challenged by the state. The defense lawyers were Samuel Leibowitz and Clarence Watts. Although Thomas Knight was the lieutenant gov-

ernor now, he was still prosecuting the case, along with
Assistant Attorney General Thomas S. Lawson.

Victoria Price took the stand and told her lies once
again. Callahan was more abusive to the defense than
ever before. He interfered with cross-examinations and
interrupted the defense lawyers with objections to their
questions. He gave the state all the leeway they wanted
though. He let the jury know how disgusted he was with
the "whole business." The trial went on for three days,
with Callahan insisting on twelve-hour days.

The jury found Haywood Patterson guilty. Nobody
was surprised by the verdict, but when they fixed his
punishment at seventy-five years, you could have heard
a pin drop. Those crackers were truly shocked that an
Alabama jury would give a Negro charged with raping a
white woman less than death.

My trial would have started the day after Haywood's,
but Callahan granted an indefinite postponement. Sam
Leibowitz requested it because one of the doctors who
was supposed to testify was sick. That day, January 24,
we were loaded into three cars for the trip back to Birmingham jail. I was put into the back seat of a car and
handcuffed to Roy Wright and Ozie Powell. I was in the
middle. A long line of cars left Decatur, with the state
highway patrol leading the way and following. Sheriff
Jay Sandlin was driving the car, and his deputy, Edgar
Blalock, was sitting beside him.

Blalock started in cussing our "Communist, Jew,
Northern lawyers." He said we'd come out a damn sight
better if we had Southern lawyers. Ozie Powell told him,
"I wouldn't give up the help I have for no damn Southern lawyer that I've seen." Blalock wheeled around and

slapped him. He didn't know that everyone of us had knives. They always searched us coming and going, and they never found our knives. We used to cut the lining in the fly of our pants and put the knives in there. They would never pat that part of us.

After slapping Ozie, Blalock said, "These sons of bitches should have been killed a long time ago—riding up and down the highway like white people." Ozie pulled out his knife, yanked Blalock's head back against the seat and slit his throat. Blood shot everywhere. The sheriff turned on the siren to draw attention from the other cars. Our car was zigzagging across the highway because the sheriff had pulled his gun and was trying to shoot into the back seat and drive too. Roy and me snatched his head back and told him he wasn't going to kill us. That's when he stopped the car. The deputy got out and staggered around to the front of the car. He flipped over on his head. The sheriff got out as a highway patrolman came running over. He said, "What the hell is going on?" The sheriff said, "One of the black bastards cut the deputy. I am going to get rid of all these sons of bitches right now!" He fired into the car and shot Ozie. The bullet went into him above his right ear and came out the corner of the automobile. As the shot was fired the lieutenant governor and assistant attorney general drove on the scene. They hollered and stopped the sheriff from shooting into the car again. Ozie was stretched out full length and his head was on my shoulder. He wasn't moving. I figgered he was dead.

Lawson told the sheriff to take the handcuffs off Ozie and rush him and the deputy to the hospital. Lieutenant Governor Knight said, "Let those niggers stay like they are and get the deputy to the hospital." That's what they did. Everybody got back into their cars and drove to the nearest town, Curving, Alabama. The chief of the highway patrol called the governor. The governor told him to strike out for Birmingham as fast as they could, and he would send the National Guard to meet them. Blood covered the windshield and it was all over the hood of the car. He figgered the people in the town would find out what was happening and form a mob to kill us.

Thomas G. Knight, the lieutenant governor of the state of Alabama, elected official and sworn to uphold the law, said, "Take these goddamn niggers over to the jail, leave the doors open and let the mob get them." He had been prosecuting the case for so many years, he saw a way to get rid of us once and for all. The chief said, "Naw, Mr. Knight, the governor gave me orders to see that these boys get to Birmingham and not to stop between here and there."

The sheriff of Curving took the place of Blalock in our car. The man who shot Ozie was still driving. He said, "You reckon anybody in Curving has got wind of this?" The other sheriff answered, "No, because they would have overtaken us by now." Sandlin was driving as slow as he could. He said, "Well, when we get over in these mountains I am going to kill the rest of these niggers." The other guy said, "That is a hard proposition you will be up against, so you'd better get yourself together." He talked to him and calmed him down.

Ozie Powell, still handcuffed to me, wasn't moving. We both were bloody as could be. All of a sudden he became conscious and said, "I ain't never been shot before."

Sheriff Sandlin yelled, "Goddamn, he's still alive. I thought I had killed him." He sounded as though he wanted to cry about it.

We finally made it to the Birmingham jail. Sandlin told us to get out of the car. Now Ozie is handcuffed to me and he can't move. Roy got out and I got out, dragging Ozie, but he was still in the car. The sheriff took his feet and shoved Ozie out on the ground. His weight pulled me and Roy down on top of him. The sheriff released the handcuffs and took me and Roy into the jail. Ozie was left laying in the yard.

When we got inside there was a bunch of reporters waiting for us. "What happened, who did what? Tell us what happened?" We did not say a word. The reporters asked us why we weren't talking. We stayed clammed up because we knew if we said one thing they would say you said something else anyway. The sheriff told the keepers to lock us up separately in solitary.

Leibowitz was on his way back to New York City and was somewhere in Tennessee when he heard the news on his car radio. He turned around and came back to Alabama. He got to see us the next day. I told him exactly what went down. Sheriff Sandlin had lied and said we tried to escape. Now how in hell were we going to escape? Just us three, handcuffed together, with a string of cars in front and back of us. All of them loaded down with guns of all kinds. How were we going to escape? One of the damndest lies ever told.

Leibowitz told us Ozie had been taken to the hospital. The governor called there and told the doctors that if they had ever saved a man to be sure and save that boy. The doctors gave him the best of attention. When they got through with him, they said Ozie stood as much chance to live as he did to die. That is, a fifty-fifty chance. They said if the bullet had gone any higher into his brain, he would have been a goner. Ozie was lucky enough to recuperate. He was charged with assault and attempted murder. He was never the same as he was, not as bright or intelligent. When we went to the penitentiary after our sentences were commuted to life, one of the stinking guards hit him in the head with a bat as we were lining up to go to breakfast. He was really a little off after that. He had brain damage of some kind. It was a goddamn shame.

CHAPTER TEN

Final Verdict

People had the notion that our being in jail stopped us from knowing what was happening on the outside. They thought we were too ignorant to know what was going on, but we knew. Some of the boys could read really well and I could understand everything concerning the case. There were newspaper articles, letters and visitors. We would discuss the case and try to decipher what was to be our fate. We knew Alabama was tired of spending thousands of dollars to prosecute us and the public was sick of the whole thing because of the bad publicity directed toward the state. Everybody wanted a resolution.

Dr. Allan Knight Chalmers was the pastor of the Broadway Tabernacle Church in New York City. A group was formed called the Scottsboro Defense Committee, and Dr. Chalmers was the chairman. The SDC consisted of representatives from nine organizations, such as the NAACP, the ILD, the American Civil Liberties

Union, the National Urban League, the League for Industrial Democracy and the Methodist Federation for Social Service. Dr. W.E.B. DuBois, Adam Clayton Powell, Jr., actor Charles Bickford, Louise Thompson, Helen Phelps Stokes and James Weldon Johnson were on the committee. Their purpose was to get as much support as possible from influential Southerners to put pressure on Alabama's officials and persuade them to reach a compromise that would set us free.

Dr. Chalmers was one of the best people on the topside of the earth. He was what a Christian should be. He stuck with us all the way. When everyone else had given up hope for us, he kept plugging away. We could always depend on him, for years after the final verdict. He visited us often, two or three times a year, always with encouraging words. He got outstanding educated people in Alabama, legislators, ex-congressmen and senators, teachers and professors, to send petitions to the governor asking for our release. I kept up a correspondence with him until he passed on. He made me believe I would be free some day. He worked like a demon to make it happen.

In December of 1936 the attorney general of Alabama, Albert Carmichael, and Lieutenant Governor Knight met with Leibowitz in New York. They talked about dropping the charges against Olen Montgomery and Willie Roberson, the boys that were sick when we were arrested, and the two youngest ones, Roy Wright and Eugene Williams. The rest of us were to plead guilty to a lesser charge and have the time we had already served applied to the sentence. They promised we would be released very soon. They couldn't get hanging Judge Callahan to go along with it though. He said we would

168

be tried for rape in his courtroom and nothing else. Nobody asked us, but we wouldn't have pleaded guilty to nothing we hadn't done.

Thomas G. Knight dropped dead in July of 1937, a few days before the last trials. By catering to the redneck lynchers in his determination to send us to the electric chair, Knight became lieutenant governor. From this office he continued to come into the courtroom as our prosecutor. His goal was to live in the governor's mansion. Had he lived, no doubt he would have made it, using the Scottsboro Case as his stepping-stone.

I went on trial for the last time July 12, 1937. Leibowitz and Clarence Watts of Huntsville defended me. The prosecution was conducted by Assistant Attorney General Thomas Lawson and H. G. Bailey, the Jackson County solicitor who prosecuted us at the trials in Scottsboro.

The weather was hot as hell. The courtroom was like a steam bath and Mr. Watts collapsed. Leibowitz had to carry on alone. A lot of people have said Leibowitz should have handled himself differently, but I don't understand that. He told the truth when he called Victoria Price a liar and a harlot. He was right when he said the Alabama juries were ignorant racists. I was proud to have him for a lawyer. If he had kissed everybody's ass down there the results would have been the same. He did his job and he proved time after time that we were innocent. I have nothing but respect for him.

Victoria Price took the stand and told her tired old lies. When Leibowitz cross-examined her, he was without mercy. A child would have known she was lying. She contradicted herself and every other sentence was "I don't know" or "I can't recollect." Leibowitz put two witnesses on the stand to testify as to Victoria's character. These men were a sheriff and a deputy from her hometown of Huntsville. They had known her since she was a teenager. The sheriff said he wouldn't believe a word she said if she was standing on a stack of Bibles. The deputy testified she was "completely untrustworthy." It was a shock to me and most all the spectators to hear this kind of testimony from Southern white men in favor of a black man against one of their own, even if true.

My trial ended July 15. The jury was out only a couple of hours before they found me guilty and I was sentenced to death once more.

The state did not ask for the death penalty in the rest of the trials. Andy Wright received ninety-nine years. Charlie Weems got seventy-five years. The rape charges against Ozie Powell was dropped and he pleaded guilty to cutting Deputy Blalock. He was given twenty years for assault.

It was July 24 when Leibowitz, Lawson and Judge Callahan went into a huddle around the bench. The next thing I knew Olen Montgomery, Willie Roberson, Eugene Williams and Roy Wright had walked out of the courtroom with Leibowitz. They got into two automobiles and left Alabama. Just like that, four of the boys were free.

I never understood it, and nobody ever explained it to me. But it was clear Leibowitz had made a deal with Alabama to free four of us, leave me behind with the death sentence and the rest with long prison terms. How could that happen? Here we were, all charged with the same offense and going through hell together for almost seven years. Suddenly, four of us are innocent enough to

170

go completely free. It was the saddest day of my life. I couldn't believe it. The worst thing was nobody explained nothing to the rest of us. Not one word from Leibowitz or anybody else. He took off with Roy, Eugene, Olen and Willie, and they headed for New York City.

The next few days the newspapers were full of it. Who made the deal? When was the deal made? How did they decide which ones should go free? Weren't we either all guilty or all innocent? The attorney general's office issued a statement that the five left behind were clearly guilty but the four that were freed had been the victims of mistaken identity. If that was true why had they been kept in jail for six and a half years? If Victoria Price was mistaken about some of the boys, all that time, how could the state credit her with being sure about me and the others? We were all charged with the same evidence. Ozie Powell was still in jail but only for assaulting the deputy; the rape charges against him were dropped. If five of us were innocent of rape, four of us couldn't be guilty.

Dr. Chalmers was in Europe when he heard the news. He returned to Alabama and requested a meeting with Governor Bibb Graves. The governor granted an interview on December 21 to Dr. Chalmers, Dr. Henry Edmonds, a Birmingham minister, and Grover Hill, editor of the Montgomery *Advertiser*. This was the memorandum of the conference:

Dr. Chalmers asked for definite action leading to the immediate release of the defendants, the details of the procedure to be left to the Governor's judgment. This act would meet with nearly unanimous approval of the press and informed public opinion, redounding to the credit of the Governor and the State of Alabama and was justified under the circumstances.

The Governor stated that he felt the position of the State was untenable, that either all were guilty or all should be free, that half fish and half fowl was not reasonable.

He said that his own mind was therefore clear on the action he should take when the cases "fell in his lap."

He felt it was not possible for him to take any action so long as there was any appeal pending before the courts, but that when the cases had been decided in the Supreme Courts and legal action had ceased, it was his intention to act quickly and definitely.

Dr. Chalmers offered to withdraw the appeals if it would facilitate the Governor's immediate action.

The Governor stated that the cases would be heard in January, that only a few weeks remained to put them before him in regular order, that he would prefer to await action until the cases had passed through their routine.

He then leaned forward and stated, "I cannot make any promise which would look like a deal. I have already stated my feeling that the position of the State is untenable with half out and half in on the same charges and evidence. My mind is clear on the action required to remedy this impossible position. When the cases come before me I intend to act promptly. I cannot be any clearer than that, can I?"

The conference lasted nearly an hour. It was

agreed by Dr. Edmonds, Grover Hall and Dr. Chalmers in an immediate consultation afterwards that their understanding was that the Governor intended to use the power vested in his office for immediate release of the accused as soon as the matter was out of the judiciary and in the hands of the executive.

The Alabama Supreme Court affirmed my execution and set the date for August 19, 1938. The same day, June 16, 1938, the court upheld the prison sentences of Andy Wright and Charlie Weems. Our lawyers didn't appeal to the United States Supreme Court because that court had decided in October of 1937 not to review Haywood Patterson's seventy-five-year conviction. Besides, Governor Graves had promised to pardon us if we were still in jail after exhausting all our legal avenues to freedom. He commuted my death sentence to life in prison July 5. A couple of weeks later I was transferred to the prison population at Kilby to begin serving a life term.

Dr. Chalmers was assured by the governor that all of us except Ozie Powell would be released October 31, 1938. We were to be on parole for six months, then we'd be on our own. Our relatives prepared places for us to live, either with them or near by. The SDC would act as our guardian and provide the opportunity for us to go to school, learn a trade and otherwise be rehabilitated.

Dr. Chalmers and Morris Shapiro, secretary of the SDC, detailed the plans to get us safely out of Alabama, once we were let go. Dr. Chalmers was to be at the prison that morning and travel with us from Montgomery to Atlanta by chauffeured limousine. We'd be met there by Mr. Shapiro, and all of us would board a train for the trip north. A stateroom was reserved for Andy,

Charlie, Haywood and me. We were to stay locked in there until out of danger. All of these efforts were in vain. The governor had no intentions of pardoning us at all.

On October 29, a Sunday, Graves interviewed us in his office, one by one. I was the last to see him. He asked me was my name Clarence Norris.

I said, "Yes, sir."

He said, "Were you on that freight train in 1931 on the 25th of March?"

I replied, "Yes, sir, I was in a fight on the train."

He asked, "Did you see any women on that freight train?"

I answered, "No, sir."

His next question I had been waiting for. "Didn't you see those other boys rape those women?"

I said, "No, sir."

He said, "I am trying to help you. I saved your life. I didn't have to do it. I could have let you go to the electric chair."

I stood there and didn't say a word.

He said, "I don't believe you have told me the truth."

I said, "Governor, I have told you the truth. I am not going to lie on the rest of the boys to save myself. I am not going to do it."

He ordered the guard to take me to my cell and told me I would hear from him soon.

That evening he sent a telegram to Dr. Chalmers and told him not to come for us because he had changed his mind. His statement to the newspapers was that he refused to pardon us because we were all sassy to him. He claimed a knife was found on Haywood Patterson.

Governor Bibb Graves was a damn liar. He reneged on

his promise to Dr. Chalmers and he lied to the public. There was too much at stake not to be on our best behavior when we saw the governor. He had our freedom in his hands and we wanted it.

Dr. Chalmers continued to plead for our release. Through Mrs. Eleanor Roosevelt he persuaded the President to invite Governor Graves to his Warm Springs home. The governor did not go.

In consequence President Roosevelt sent the governor a letter. He wrote that he was sorry the governor couldn't make the trip. He said it was well known the governor had given his word to "definitely and positively commute the sentences of the remainder of the Scottsboro Boys." He said he feared Graves would "lose many friends" if he went back on his promise.

The governor of Alabama was not moved. Haywood Patterson was transferred to the Atmore Prison Farm, said to be the worst penal institution in the South. Andy, Charlie, Ozie and me settled into the penitentiary life at Kilby.

CHAPTER ELEVEN

Life Sentence

Five thousand men lived in Kilby Prison, sometimes a few hundred more, sometimes a few hundred less. The number of black inmates tripled the amount of white prisoners. The building we were housed in was made of red brick and was six stories high. Inside it was like a square beehive made of steel doors and bars. Rows of cells stretched along the walls all the way around. The white inmates had cells all to themselves. Cells on the black side were packed all the time with as many as ten men to a cell. The white inmates' cells were on one side of the building, and blacks lived on the other side.

It took a long time to be able to get any kind of sleep. There was noise all night long—screams, moans and groans. The cockroaches were as big as my thumbs and they moved in armies. They bit us along with the millions of bedbugs. The scratching that went on echoed in the night. Everybody had body crabs and lice. Mice ran through the cells like pets.

I have been asked if I believe in God and Heaven and Hell. Do I believe in Christianity? Am I a Christian? I know the legislators who let Kilby exist would say they were Christians. The judges and prosecutors who tried to frame me out of my life said they were Christians too. I believe if there is a God He forgot about me and my companions in the case. I don't know about Heaven but there damn sure is a Hell. I lived there from 1938 until 1946.

First I was taken to Warden William's office. He did all the talking. "You are out of the death cells but your sentence has been commuted to life in prison. I don't care why you are here. I don't have anything to do with it. I don't know if you are guilty or not guilty. I am here to do a job. I have but one rule and that's *do right!* You can pick a good or a bad crowd to associate with but if you want to do right, you had better pick the right crowd."

I was taken to the psychiatrist to be classed in a job category. He asked me different questions, but there wasn't much to it. He didn't care whether I was crazy or not. I was given an eye test and my reflexes were examined. I was classed for the cotton mill. I was glad not to be classed for farming or for factory labor, but the mill was no picnic. There was a TB hospital on the prison grounds because so many got tuberculosis working in the cotton mill. Breathing all the lint and dust ate up their lungs.

The cotton mill was big business for the state. There was a dye shop, spinning room, weave shop and sewing room. The cotton was dyed, made into thread, spooled and stretched, then woven into cloth. The cloth was shipped everywhere in this country and to foreign places.

178

Shirts were made in bulk, some for prisoners but most for private concerns. The labels of these companies were sewed on the shirts and cloth in the prison.

The sewing room was set up so each man made a certain part of the shirt. The collars, cuffs, backs and fronts. After he is broken into this work, a man had to produce so many dozen an hour. If he didn't make his quota he was punished. When anybody messed up his task or tried to shirk it he was beaten. They'd be taken to the front and you could hear the whips whistling and the screams. This went on in all the work areas. Everybody had to do their jobs to the satisfaction of the guards and bossmen.

The bells started ringing at four in the morning to get us up for breakfast. The dining room was a separate building on the grounds. The dining room was divided by a partition to separate black and white prisoners. We were forbidden to eat with the white prisoners. For one thing they didn't want us to see the better food the white prisoners received. I seldom went to the dining room. The stuff they passed off as food wasn't fit for hogs. It was beans, greens, grits, and old bread. We never got meat, fish or fowl. The food smelled bad, looked terrible and had to be forced down. I paid the cooks three dollars a week, as I had in Birmingham, to get decent meals. They sent my food to my cell and on my job. I ate whatever the guards were served, milk, eggs, ham, beefsteaks, even desserts.

At six o'clock we had better be in that line to be counted into our work details, headed for the cotton mill, the canning factory or the farm. Kilby had hundreds of acres that were used for farming. Cotton was the big crop but convicts planted, tended and harvested rice, okra, corn, tomatoes, sweet potatoes, cucumbers, green beans, squash, onions, you name the vegetable. There were groves of pecan and fruit trees too. None of it found its way into the dining room. The farmers were searched every evening before they got back to their cells. They would be severely punished if caught with a few tomatoes or nuts.

It was all to be sold to private industry. What they didn't sell fresh was canned in the factory. The cans were labeled and sent all over the country. Every few years there would be a scandal about where all the money was going. We earned fifteen cents a week, after working six days, twelve hours a day. On Saturday as we were counted back into the cell block, there was two guards at the head of the line. Each had a sack of coins. One guard would hand us a nickel, and the other gave us a dime.

I operated several machines in the mill. My job was to turn the dyed cotton into thread. All those years I always operated machinery of one kind or another. I lost my finger one Monday morning in the fall of 1939. The captain told me to clean my machines. All the guards were addressed as captain. I had cleaned the machines before, but this particular morning I must have been deep into thinking about my troubles. Some parts of the machine I cut off and some parts I had to keep running, so the thread was always being made. There was a section of the machine that I thought I had turned off but I didn't. I saw a piece of cotton down in a little hole and I stuck my finger in there to get the cotton out. My finger was sliced clean through.

I lost my finger down to the second knuckle. The doctor didn't sew it up the way he should have and after the stitches came out, my finger opened up again. Blood poisoning set in it, and I was in the hospital about four weeks.

All the prisoners were insured by the state. Since I got hurt on the job I was entitled to compensation. But for a long time none of the blacks knew we could get money for these injuries. A guy who was a lifer and a trusty told me about' it. He slipped letters out to a lawyer in Montgomery and asked him to help me and others to get our money. Sure enough, the lawyer came out to Kilby. I was taken along with twelve other guys to an office in Montgomery. We were asked how many limbs and joints we had lost. I had lost a joint and a half off my finger. Everybody got a settlement but me. They told me I couldn't get anything because the guards said I hurt myself intentionally.

I was treated that way because I was a Scottsboro Boy. They figured the state had spent enough money on us. As Scottsboro defendants we always got the dirty end of the stick. Five days after Charlie Weems started serving his seventy-five years, a guard attacked him with a baling hook, ripped Charlie's chest open and cut his throat. He was hospitalized for months in a serious condition. The guard was suspended for a time, then he was back on the job. The governor reinstated him. After the loss of my finger I was put back to work on the same machines. I learned to be very careful when I cleaned them.

In prison your life is in danger at all times. Somebody got killed practically every day. I never heard of a black prisoner killing a white prisoner or vice versa. Blacks killed blacks and whites killed whites. The guards killed anybody. The guards were the biggest hazard around.

Most of them were half crazy with hate and full of prejudices against blacks and convicts. They were the worst sort of redneck, ignorant, uneducated cracker. The language they spoke isn't fit to be repeated. But all I heard all day long was "black-ass nigger" and "black son of a bitch." The hardest-working, model prisoner couldn't escape their mistreatment. They were like wild animals turned loose on helpless unarmed people.

Most of the killing between the inmates was about the girl-boys, gambling or money. You could get killed quick about some money. The girl-boys were men who were used as women. This is just part of penitentiary life. Some men will turn into women once they get in prison. Most of them were youngsters who didn't have anyone to send them anything. The older inmates took advantage of them. The men that preyed on the young boys were called wolves. They would befriend the boys and offer them money and cigarettes. If they accepted these gifts, the boys would have only one way to pay up. Some of the youngsters ended up selling their bodies like prostitutes. They would dress as women with powder and lipstick.

A lot of raping went on too. The wolves would walk into a boy's cell or trap him in the bathroom. They'd have a homemade knife called a dutch. The boy would be asked if he wanted the dick or the dutch. The boys would be scared and go along with it; some of them would kill or die first; some would holler for the guards. That was a terrible thing for a fella to get on his record. Rape or attempted rape. If a boy called the guards he was usually killed and nobody would know nothing.

No matter if he was raped, became a prostitute or gave in to a particular wolf, the boy was known as a girl-boy

182

from then on. The girl-boys kept the men stirred up all the time. The men involved were constantly going before the warden to be disciplined for fighting, stabbings and suspicion of murder. You can't survive in prison that way. The girl-boys killed their men because that was the only way to get rid of them when they got tired. The men killed each other out of jealousy or somebody trying to take their girl-boy from them. The men would sell their girl-boys, sometimes for as much as a hundred dollars. Then they couldn't touch the girl-boy any more or they would be killed. That homosexual shit kept bodies falling all the time.

The trusties had a good business selling Vaseline. A large jar cost about thirty cents but they could get from twenty to thirty dollars for it. The trusties bought it on the outside, cut it with lard, put it into snuff cans and sold the cans for a dollar apiece.

If the guards caught the men fucking, they would be given up to ninety days in the hole plus a beating. Lots of inmates were tangled in homosexual relationships. You had to be strong because if you showed the slightest weakness you would be forced to get involved. Once involved, your life wasn't worth two dead flies. Your record was shot and you could forget about pardons and parole. I wouldn't risk my freedom for that kind of thing. I tried to stay out of trouble and abide by the rules. It wouldn't do me any good to try and be a tough guy. I had to keep a level head, know who to associate with and keep my eyes open for whatever might happen.

Once I took a piece of scrap cloth that had been thrown in the garbage. It was seconds. I was going to use it to gamble on. It was rolled up, and I didn't know how many yards I had. I walked into the cell block with this cloth under my arm. The guard snatched the material and unfolded it; there must have been six yards. He took me to the warden.

The warden said, "Clarence how long have you been in prison?" I told him eleven years. He said, "You've been a prisoner for a long time and you'll be coming up for parole soon. I'd like to see you free, so I am going to ignore this incident. It won't go on your record." I thanked him. He told me not to come before him again. I said I would do my best. There was nothing I could have done with that cloth and it was being thrown away, but the dirty guard tried to make something out of it and get me into trouble.

The first fight I had in prison was about gambling. A guy owed me some money and refused to pay me. We fought, but the guards didn't see us, so we were not punished. I beat this guy pretty badly, and he laid for me. I knew it was only a matter of time before he'd try and get his revenge. Days passed until one evening I was leaving the job and he jumped me. He sneaked from behind a door and tried to bust me in the head with an iron roller. I saw him just as he was swinging, and I ducked so he only hit me on the shoulder. I grabbed the roller and tried to kill him.

The guards broke up the fight. They took us down to the hole. Each of us had to drink a cup of castor oil. We were given belts and told to beat each other until one of us dropped. We did this but we both fell out. They locked us in separate cells. When they closed the door on me down there in the hole, I couldn't see my hands before my eyes. I didn't know night from day. They gave me a bucket to use for my toilet. I had plenty of use for it because of the castor oil. I went to the bucket until I was weak. It was four days before they let me dump that bucket. My bed was the concrete floor and a blanket. Each day I was given a piece of bread and a cup of water. That's it! I was in there for ten days. Guys who went to the hole for thirty, sixty and ninety days would be skeletons when they got out. They would have to be taken to the hospital and nursed back to health. Too many times, too long in there, a man would never be the same. Many prisoners went from the hole to the crazy house or to the grave.

They had a whipping rule. If you did something against the rules, it was taken up before the board of corrections and they decided what type of punishment you should have. You could get as many as twenty-five lashes. The second time I was punished for fighting I received ten lashes. I was stretched out on my stomach on the floor. A guard sat on my shoulders and one on each of my legs. They didn't ask me to remove my pants because the whip ripped them, my underwear and my skin wide open, the first blow. It was like being struck with a razor blade. The first lash felt as though a building had fell on me. After the third lash I didn't know where I was or what happened. When I came to myself the doctor had put pads and bandages on my backside. Almost forty years later I still carry the scars.

There was a dirty white prisoner on my job who kept asking me if I raped those women. The only time I was around white prisoners was on the job. I told him to leave me alone. He kept asking me the same damn thing until I told him that I didn't tell the judge I did it, and I sure as hell wasn't going to tell him no different. This pissed him off. I had a job then where all I had to do was watch twelve machines and keep them running. If something went wrong with them they would automatically stop. I would find the trouble and fix it. I sat there all day and watched these machines. I was sitting down with another guy, a white prisoner, who was a mechanic. We had the same job, but they called him a mechanic. All of a sudden my machines started to make a terrible noise. I jumped up to see what the matter was, and I found rocks in the machines. The guard wanted to know how the rocks got in there.

The cracker who had been questioning me and pestering me came running up. He was hollering, "That nigger did it, I seen him do it." The mechanic I had been sitting with told the guard I couldn't have done it because my machines had been running smoothly and he had been with me all the time. The other prisoner was screaming, "I saw him. I saw him put those rocks in there." The guard asked him what the hell he was doing over there, it wasn't his department. They took the son of a bitch to the hole and kept him on bread and water for ninety days. That's what you got for destroying state property.

I was scared because I figgered when he got out he'd get a bunch of his friends and try to kill me in the yard one day. When he surfaced again he was damn near dead. I never had any trouble from that quarter again. I was lucky. If it hadn't been for that other white convict, I would have had it. He could have been the type to stand by his color in a lie and not said a thing. In prison they always took a white man's word over a black's every time, just like in the free streets.

I had a headache one morning and went to the place called the sick hall. You could report there in the morning or in the afternoon if anything was wrong with you. There were white prisoners that worked there who treated you for sickness. They claimed to have worked in hospitals or doctor's offices when they were free. They walked around in white clothes and some of them were pretty good. I told one I had a headache and he handed me what he said were a couple of aspirins. I took what he gave me and for two days I spit up until there was nothing but water coming out of me. I was sick to my stomach and couldn't eat. I got weaker and weaker. Finally I was so sick on the job, the guard took me to the hospital. The doctor asked me what was the matter and I told him what had happened. He gave me a shot of some kind and made me drink a lot of water. I sat there for a while before I started throwing up. I gagged and gagged. I was so weak I couldn't walk and they had to carry me to a bed. I was in the hospital for damn near three weeks. That sick hall worker had tried to poison me. I heard the doctor raising hell with him about it. Those weren't no aspirins that cracker gave me. I never knew what made him do it but it was probably because those women said we raped them.

The officials tried to keep the races from mixing with each other. After work and all day Sunday, all the inmates were allowed to go to the yard. We could sit in the sun, throw a ball around, play games and amuse ourselves as best we could. The blacks were expected to stay on their side of the yard, but blacks and whites got together anyway, different people did. Every now and then there was some racial trouble, then everybody stayed on their side of the yard until things cooled down.

Once there was an incident and the governor came to Kilby to talk to us about it. Governor Graves stood on a platform in the dining room. He gave a speech and in it he said, "The lowest white man is better than the highest-class Negro who ever lived." The white prisoners cheered for a long while. He had given them a license to kill. This man held the highest office in the state and had sworn to uphold the law. I went back to my cell and thought about the man who had my freedom in his hands.

A lot of prisoners don't give a damn if they live or die. These are people to avoid. It only takes a few prisoners to start serious trouble that can get you killed. Riots and protests come about because the authorities are cruel. When men are treated like dirt, worked to death, paid nothing and fed slop, they are a powder keg. One afternoon some fellas decided to pull a strike about the food. I didn't know nothing about it and neither did most of us. It began at lunchtime. Word was passed for everybody to go into the yard. A group of black and white prisoners started the thing. They yelled for nobody to go into the dining room or the cell blocks. The National Guard came out of nowhere and surrounded the cotton mill. This was so nobody could get in there and destroy the machines.

When an uprising comes along in an institution, you are just in it. It doesn't matter if you want to be or not, because there are only two sides, the inmates and the officials. The guards fired over the heads of the guys who were raising all the hell. The bullets made chips of brick fly off the buildings and walls. A lot of us weren't close enough to really know what was going on. I thought they were shooting gas. The guards ordered everybody into the cell blocks. Nobody moved. The guards shot directly into the crowd. Quite a few guys were hit, I could see the blood. The guards in the gun towers fired on us. Bodies began to fall. Five thousand men tried to get into the cell block at the same time. They were stampeding like cattle. I was knocked down and trampled. Every time I tried to get up, I was run over. I finally grabbed ahold to somebody's belt and the crowd pulled me up. Somehow I made it back to my cell.

The guards came around to the cells to see who was hurt and needed to be taken to the hospital. Nobody was killed and that was a surprise to me. I went to the hospital because the skin on my knees and elbows was torn to pieces. I had to laugh at some of the fellas in the hospital. One guy had sand in his eyes and he was so pitiful it was funny to me. Another fella called himself a preacher, and when the riot started he was carrying his Bible. He sat off in a corner to keep from getting mixed up in anything. He got shot. He threw his Bible down and ran like hell when that bullet hit him. That was the damndest situation I have ever been in.

The worst feeling about being locked up was it didn't seem real. It was akin to living in a dream. Thinking that it will end in a minute. I had no control over what happened to me, not at all. From the time I was taken off that train, I was a robot. I was told what to do, when to do it and how. Most of the time I tried not to think of anything. Thinking and hearing about the pleasures people in the outside world were having was something I couldn't stand. If I had been an old man maybe I could have borne it better. But I was young and an innocent man besides. Sometimes I got so downhearted I thought I wouldn't be able to stand it. Then I'd get a letter bringing encouraging words and hope. I'd understand that I had to hold myself together because freedom might be near.

One of the most discouraging letters I ever received was from Joseph Brodsky. He wrote and told me how sorry he was that the case had been handled wrong and so forth. The International Labor Defense had run out of money and wasn't operating any more. It was a good organization from what I knew of it. I know I would have been a dead man a long time ago if it hadn't been for them. They went bankrupt because so many people, North and South, were against them for being Communists. The papers said they were troublemakers and the members were always going to jail. They had to pay thousands of dollars in fines to stay out of the penitentiary themselves. I know they not only tried to help us but free poor people too. The people in command didn't like that and they set out to destroy them. It was a damn shame.

As the years rocked around, the letters slowed down to a trickle compared to the earlier years. So much time passed, I guess people forgot about us or went on to other things. I still got letters from some outstanding citizens though. Bill Robinson, the dancer, wrote, so did Edward Small who owned Small's Paradise in Harlem. I got letters from the owner of the *Amsterdam News* too.

The only person who came to see me when I was serving time was Dr. Allan Knight Chalmers. He would come a couple of times a year. He and the Scottsboro Defense Committee were steady pressuring the governor and the Board of Pardons and Paroles to give us our freedom.

190

CHAPTER TWELVE

Dora Lee

All the fights, going before the warden, doing time in the hole and the whippings I took happened during the first half of 1943. I had been in jail for twelve years. I was tired of being in the penitentiary for nothing. The years passing me by and my young manhood slipping away was getting too much for me. I began to lose hope; without hope a man in prison is nothing. My mind and body was breaking under the strain of wondering if my innocence would ever be proved. I was helpless and couldn't do it myself. I had to depend on Dr. Chalmers, the Scottsboro Defense Committee, the NAACP and all the others to keep their promise of freedom. They had to stay on the backs of the parole board and the governor or we'd never get out. I never knew much about what the people on the outside were doing to free us after my sentence was commuted to life. I just kept hoping they wouldn't get tired.

In October of 1943 the pardons and paroles board

came out to talk with me. They told me I was eligible for a parole. They asked me where I'd like to go if I got the parole. I asked them to send me to Cleveland, Ohio, because my mother was there. They said they would arrange that for me if the Ohio parole authorities would accept me and if a job could be found for me.

Back in my cell, I wrote Dr. Chalmers about the interview. I told him I didn't want to be paroled to a Southern state. I asked him to help me get to Cleveland or New York.

Roy Wilkins, then assistant secretary of the NAACP, got me a job in Cleveland paying forty dollars a week. The Alabama board claimed the environment in Cleveland wouldn't be a fit place for me because the man my mother had married was serving a life sentence in the Ohio penitentiary for murder. Mr. Wilkins wrote the board that the NAACP would hire me as a shipping clerk in their New York office. The New York parole authorities approved my coming there but Alabama wouldn't.

Charlie Weems was released in November of '43 and paroled to Atlanta, Georgia. Andy Wright and me could have been paroled too, but we stayed in prison because we wouldn't accept parole in the South.

An old guy named Jack Lindsay who had been a deputy warden at Kilby became the parole agent in Montgomery. He was one of the filthiest, lowdown men who ever lived. He told the Alabama board he had jobs for us in Montgomery. Andy and me were told this was the only place the board would approve our going. We refused.

A couple of weeks went by. I said to Andy, "I don't give a damn where we are paroled. I just want to hit the

192

free streets." He said, "They will force us to take parole in Alabama now." "We don't have to stay, we'll be free." I talked Andy into taking the parole.

January 6, 1944, Jack Lindsay drove us to the Foshee Lumber Company. It might as well have been a prison camp. The place was owned by a man named Easley. He had built all these little houses and most of his employees lived on the premises. So we paid our salaries back to him in rent. The pay was thirty-five cents an hour. The rent was seven dollars a week.

This was my first freedom in thirteen years. Our rules were we couldn't drink, keep late hours or leave the vicinity. Lindsay took us to the woman's house who sold meals to the workers, then he left.

The woman said, "I have been reading about you boys for a long time and I sure am glad to see you free."

She brought out a quart of Scotch liquor. "Would you boys like a drink?" We said no.

"Go on and drink. I know what the rules are. Don't worry about me telling that parole bastard nothing." She went out of the room. I looked at the bottle and I looked at Andy. "Andy, you going to take a drink?" Andy said, "You think she's trying to get us back in prison?" "I don't know but I'm out here supposed to be free and I'm going to take one." I took a glass, poured a big drink and downed it. Andy said, "I might as well have one too." I said, "We have broken our parole already." We sat there drinking and talking to the lady. That was my first day of freedom.

Thirty-five cents an hour ain't nothing. They took out income tax too. I had never heard of tax before. I got my first check and I asked Andy about the deductions. He said I had to state my dependents. He explained to me

193

what dependents were and I went running to the boss. I told the man, "I got dependents, my mother and six sisters." I put them all down. They didn't deduct nothing after that.

The NAACP sent Andy and me checks for two hundred dollars apiece to buy clothes. That's when I had one of the most heartbreaking experiences of my life. We went into town to buy suits. Andy found a suit he liked and bought it without incident. I found the suit I wanted at another store. I tried it on and gave my two hundred dollar check to the owner. He looked at the check and said, "Oh, so you're one of those Scottsboro Boys."

I said yes.

He wrapped up the suit and handed me my change. The suit cost sixty dollars. I was halfway out of the store, counting the change, and I saw he had made a mistake. I said, "Mister, this is not the right money." He hollered at me, "Get the hell out of here nigger, you've got all the change you're gonna get from me." Andy grabbed me and pulled me out of the door. Outside Andy was holding onto me. Tears of madness were rolling down my face. "I'm going to kill him Andy, I've got to kill him." "No, Clarence, if you do they will get a chance to do what they have wanted to all these years. He's got a gun in there, and he is itching to use it on you." Andy was raging at me.

I have never felt so helpless as then. The son of a bitch stole my money. It never entered my mind to call the police. I just went on. But I wanted to murder.

I was determined to stay free and make good. I wanted to prove to everybody who had helped me I was worthy of their support all those years. But it was an impossible task. Andy and I were treated as dogs. It was worse than prison because the condition we lived under wasn't what freedom should be.

Andy and me shared a room, eight by ten feet, and we had to sleep in the same bed, with one pillow. We were assigned the hardest work. The foreman cussed us all the time. He kept asking us, "Didn't you have those women?" They wanted us to do something that would get them stirred up enough to lynch us. Or get us to attack them so they'd have an excuse to kill us. I was walking on eggs all the time. I believe the Alabama board wanted us paroled in the South so they could embarrass the people who had worked for our freedom ... Dr. Chalmers in particular. That's why they tied us to that state. They knew it would be very hard for us to stay out of trouble.

One Sunday I went down to Dix Avenue to a movie. When I left the movie, I caught a bus. Blacks and whites rode the bus together, but we had to sit in the back. If the bus was loaded, every time a white person got on, a black person had to give up his seat and go further in the back to stand. We'd be packed in the back of the damn bus like sardines in a can. After most of the white people had got off this bus, we were in the colored neighborhood. World War Two was going on and women had started wearing slacks. A black woman got on the bus wearing pants. She took the first seat she found vacant.

"Get up from there, nigger boy, you don't sit there." She said, "Mister, I am not a boy, I am a lady." The driver said, "I don't give a damn what you are, get up and move your black ass to the rear." She said, "Give me my money back." "I am not going to give you a damn thing, get off my bus." The woman got off.

My heart bled. The bus drivers carried guns in those

days just like the police. I said to myself, how cowardly can we be? If that had been a black driver (which was unheard of) who had put a white woman off or talked to her that way, he would have been killed for sure. When all the white people were off the bus, the driver said, "How come somebody didn't tell me that was a colored girl?" Nobody said a word. He didn't care that she was a lady or a man. Colored was the thing important to him.

I met a beautiful woman named Dora Lee. She stayed with her aunt on the lumber company grounds. We began to see a lot of each other. When we met she had been seeing another fellow. One night I was taking her to the movies. The moon was shining so bright. Do you know how the moon shines in the South? It is quite a sight! We were strolling along and her ex drove up. "Come here," he called to Dora. She didn't want to go over to the car, but I told her to see what he wanted. She went over, and the guy tried to force her into the car. I ran over and said, "Man are you crazy, don't never disrespect this woman. You had best keep on driving. If you don't like what I'm saying, do something about it right now." He took off.

This man worked on the same job as me. He operated some machinery. One day I went to see Dora and he was in the backyard with her. He was threatening her and demanding that she come back to him. He saw me and started telling me how long they had gone out together and he wasn't going to give her up. I told him she was going with me now and I didn't force her to do it. I asked him to leave her alone. We had a big fuss before he left. This was a married man, living with his wife. From that day, he didn't speak to me on the job any more. His brother worked for the lumber company too. He was a decent fellow. He told me he had a fool for a brother.

Dora Lee

Dora Lee and I were married the third Sunday in March 1944, before a preacher. My wife was twenty years old and I was thirty-one. We moved off the lumber company property and rented a two-room house on Oak Street. Dora was a cook, she cooked in white folks' houses. I wanted to change my job so I could make more money. It was wartime and there was lots of good jobs available. Most men were making from seventy-five cents to a dollar an hour on any kind of a job. But my boss refused to pay me more and the parole agent wouldn't allow me to change jobs. I couldn't get any satisfaction. I complained to my boss, the parole agent and the board. Jobs were plentiful because the war was on. Why did I have to work for pennies? Why did I have to get permission to change my job and I was a free man? The more I complained the harsher my boss treated me. Finally Lindsay said I could change jobs but I had to go to another lumber company. I went because I got a big, fat, nickel raise. I figured forty cents an hour was better than thirty-five. I was wrong. Marshall Lumber Company was a natural chain gang. The bosses really hard-timed me and gave me the filthy work.

Dr. Chalmers came to visit me and to meet my wife. He told us he was working to get me transferred to Cleveland. Dr. Chalmers had visited me and Andy several times that year. He always came at night. He would send a car for us. The driver took us to a beautiful house that was owned by Reverend Ralph Riley, pastor of the Dexter Avenue Baptist Church. This is the same church Dr. Martin Luther King, Jr., became minister of ten years later.

The parole people finally said the Montgomery county employment office refused to let me transfer to Ohio. They said the War Manpower Board ". . . prohibited an employee of an industry classed as essential to the war effort to change employment without a referral by the employment office." I quote from a letter sent to Dr. Chalmers from the Alabama board. I was already doing the worst kind of manual labor they had at Marshall's when the foreman tried to get me to start working with green lumber. I refused and went to the parole agent's office. I told him how they were doing me on that job. I explained to him that I wanted to go on a decent job; a job where I could make enough money to live decently. He said, "Not a chance."

Andy and me broke parole on the same day. He was married by then too. He wedded a woman from Mobile. Andy was a sick man with no business doing hard work. The doctor had given Andy a prescription for digitalis because he had a heart condition. Andy told his bosses and Jack Lindsay, but the bastards still would not let him change jobs or do easier work. He would probably have died if he'd stayed there.

I just couldn't take any more from those rotten crackers. I figured if I got up North the organizations would be able to pressure the state of Alabama into letting me be paroled to Cleveland or New York City. I thought if I left I'd never have to come back again. I had served so many years and suffered too much for something I had not done. I knew I'd rather die than keep living under those conditions, knowing they would probably get worse before they got better.

I took a train to New York City, September 27, 1944. I was going to send for Dora Lee as soon as I found a job and a place for us to stay. Grand Central Station was the biggest building I'd ever seen. You could put all the people in Montgomery in there.

Dora Lee

I went straight to the Broadway Tabernacle Church to see Dr. Chalmers. He wasn't there, but his secretary sent me to the office of the International Labor Defense. I met with Morris Shapiro. He took me to the home of a black lawyer on Convent Avenue in the section of Harlem called Sugar Hill. The lawyer was married to a truly beautiful woman. Their home was the prettiest I'd ever known. They made me feel at home and gave me the run of the house. I stayed there a week.

It was in all the papers: SCOTTSBORO BOY BREAKS PAROLE. Mr. Shapiro called the Alabama board and said he had read that Clarence Norris had left Alabama. I was sitting there with him when he made the call. He told them if I contacted him, he would advise me to return to Alabama, on the condition that they would see that I got a decent, better paying job and not send me back to the penitentiary. The board agreed to that. I let Roy Wilkins, Morris Shapiro and Dr. Chalmers talk me into going back to Alabama. They said they would do everything in their power to make the parole board live up to their promises. I told them that those crackers would promise anything to get me back down there. But I trusted them and went along with it.

I left New York at eight on a Friday evening and I got into Montgomery that Sunday at one o'clock in the afternoon. I spent the night with Dora Lee. I didn't report to the parole people until that Monday morning. The Board of Pardons and Paroles was made up of two men and a woman. Mrs. Mitchell did the talking: "Clarence, you left the state without permission and violated your parole. But we are not going to send you back to prison." That was music to my ears. I told them I had been in Cleveland visiting my mother.

199

They sent me to the parole agent's office. Lindsay grinned at me and said, "You think you are going on one of those jobs paying big money, but you can forget about it." He said, "Do you want to go back to your job at Marshall's or do you miss the cotton mill at Kilby Prison?" Quite naturally I said I'd go back to the lumber company. I left his office and sent a telegram to Dr. Chalmers. He answered me to try and tough it out because they were doing all possible to get me transferred out of the state.

My boss was mad as hell that I had run off. He had me stacking that green lumber and gave me the toughest jobs to do. It was "nigger this" and "nigger that." He forgot my name altogether. He kept throwing Victoria Price and Ruby Bates in my face, daring me to raise my hands to him. I was treated as a slave. I became frightened for my life.

Dora and me discussed the situation and I decided to plead with Lindsay; maybe he'd give me a break. I never can forget that morning. My wife was washing clothes. I kissed her good-bye and said I'd see her that evening. It was the last time I was to see her as a free man for two years.

I went to the parole agent's office and explained myself to him. He said, "I am sick of your complaints, I'll call the board and whatever they say is satisfactory with me." He told me to have a seat, and he went and made the phone call. Fifteen minutes later the deputy warden and the warden of Kilby Prison walked through the doorway. They slapped the handcuffs on me, shoved me in a car, drove to the prison and put me back behind the walls. It was October 18, 1944. I had been free for nine months.

200

Dora Lee

A couple of days later, the parole board came to Kilby. They said my boss told them I wouldn't work and I was absent or late all the time. That was a damn lie and I told them so. I had never been late or missed a day. They said they would review my case and I'd hear from them soon. A few weeks went by before they sent me any word. The letter said I would be reconsidered for parole again in 1946.

I was filled with rage and hatred. Going back to prison hurt me more than when I was sentenced to the chair. I missed my wife, we had only been married seven months. We were very much in love and had never had an argument. I couldn't believe what had happened to me. I could have killed every cracker in Alabama and been joyful doing it. I was sick to my soul. I did those two years and they were harder than all the thirteen that had gone before. I grieved.

I was back in the cotton mill and the prison routine. It was as if I had never been away. Dr. Chalmers visited me and told me he wouldn't give up trying to get me out again. I made a promise to myself that if I was ever freed I'd keep on getting up and nobody in Alabama or involved with the case would ever see me again.

The first year after I went back, Dora Lee came to see me every visiting day and stayed until they made her leave. Her letters came so fast I couldn't keep up with them. She wrote two and three times a week. The last time she came to the prison, she only stayed for two hours. She said her cousin was home on furlough from the army and he was staying with her. He was leaving that day and she wanted to see him off. She never visited me again.

I wrote her letters, lots of letters, but she never answered them. She sent me a package of cigarettes, lotions, face cream, toothpaste and cologne. I have always taken care of my skin just like a woman does and she knew what I used. I didn't have to shave. I didn't start shaving regularly until I was in my fifties. Anyhow, she sent the package with no letter or message of any kind.

In 1946 I was up for parole and the board came out for a visit. They had found me a job working for the gas company. They said that I'd make a good salary and there was plenty of overtime. They didn't tell me it was ditching; digging ditches for the gas lines, with a pick and shovel.

The 27th of September, 1946, I was laying on my bunk and the cons started hollering, "Clarence, you're being paroled today." At six o'clock I got in the line going to the cotton mill. The guys asked me, "Why are you going to work?" I said, "I'm not foolish enough to believe what's in the papers. When the warden tells me I'm paroled, that's where it's at." I hadn't been on the job an hour before I was called to the front. The guard told me to go to the laundry for clean clothes. They gave me a cheap suit and some old work shoes and twenty-seven dollars. I put it with the near three hundred dollars I had, my gambling winnings.

Outside the gate I was surrounded by reporters and flashbulbs going off in my face. "What you gonna do now Clarence? What are your plans?" I told them I wanted to make a decent living and live as a person should. That's all I said to them.

I took the bus into Montgomery. I bought a pair of shoes and threw away the ones I had on. I didn't need clothes, I thought Dora had probably kept those I had left with her. I hadn't seen my wife for at least a year.

So when I was released I didn't know what was happening with her.

The first thing I had to do was report to Jack Lindsay. I walked into his office and he said, "Hi, Clarence, I see you're out again. You know what to do this time, don't you?" I said, "Yes, sir, I sure do." He gave me the address to the job and directions to get there. I wasn't even listening. I knew they would not see me.

Two black men standing on the street were listening to a broadcast about me on the radio. I walked up to them and said, "That's me they're talking about." They got very excited. We shook hands all around and they gave me their phone numbers and addresses. They wanted me to go home with them and meet their families. I told them I would one day. As soon as I left them I forgot them. My mind was filled with Dora Lee.

I was heading towards our house when an old lady I knew called out hello from her porch. I walked over to her and she said, "Now Clarence, don't get yourself in any trouble, son. Dora Lee is going with one of the deacons in the church." I told her not to worry.

At the house Dora opened the door and greeted me with hugs and kisses. We ate dinner together and began to talk.

"What are you planning to do?" I asked her.

"What do you mean, Clarence?"

I said, "As far as you and I being man and wife." She shook her head for no: "I can't live with you and I'm sorry about everything." I told her, "I won't ask you why but I want you to know that I still love you." It was Thursday evening, she told me she had to visit her mother and she'd be back soon. She didn't come back until the next morning. She fixed breakfast for me and we didn't have anything to say to each other. A friend came by and he and I went out together to have a few drinks. Dora Lee was dressed to go out when I got back home. She left and I had the house to myself again that night. Saturday morning she walked in and we had breakfast in silence again. After she washed up the dishes and dusted around, straightening up the house, she took off for her mother's house. Some fellows came by and I went out with them. I didn't come back that night. Sunday morning, back home, Dora wasn't there. Late that afternoon she came in and gave me three ten-dollar bills. She told me she had money saved in the post office and she would give it to me that Monday morning. I just looked at her.

There was a big gambling game going on at the Foshee Lumber Company property. I went out there to try my luck. Everybody was glad to see me, and they told me how well I looked. I learned to gamble in prison and how to cheat too. The other guys were drinking and most of them were half drunk. It was easy for me to pull a few tricks, and I won practically every hand. When the game was over I had everybody's money and my pockets were jammed. My front pockets were full of quarters. Dora Lee's cousin, Elsie, was there, and I gave her all the change, something like twelve dollars. She asked me how Dora and I were getting along. I told her we weren't and I didn't think we could make it any more. She said she was sorry for us both.

I went home knowing my wife and her deacon were at the church. I packed up my things and waited. When she came in Dora Lee asked me if I was leaving town and I told her no. I made a little speech. "I have to find another place because I can't stand living here with you like brother and sister. I could be violent but that wouldn't do any good. I can't compel you to love me, but I hope you never treat whoever you do love the way you have treated me." I took her in my arms and kissed her. I walked out with my suitcase, and that's the last I ever saw of her.

I went by train to Atlanta, Georgia. I visited the NAACP office on Albany Avenue. The office manager was a middle-aged, settled man. He and his wife were fine people. He called Roy Wilkins in New York and told him what I had done. Roy Wilkins said I never should have left Alabama and there would be hell to pay. He said there was nothing he could do for me but he didn't tell me to go back. The manager asked me what I was going to do. I told him I was going to New York. He wrote me out a check and his wife went to the bank to cash it.

I was sitting there talking to them and I was seated next to the window. I happened to look out and I saw Charlie Weems walking by. I said excuse me and ran down the three flights of steps. I would recognize Charlie Weems anywhere. He was a tall, lanky fellow and he always held his head tilted to the side as though he had a broken neck. I ran up to him and must have scared him to death. We were very excited at seeing each other, grinning, jumping up and down and shaking hands. It was hard to believe we were both on the free streets at last. Charlie was married and he invited me to his home. I had dinner with them and spent the night. The next evening they saw me off at the train station. Charlie told me to write to him but I never did. I haven't seen or heard anything about him from that day until now.

CHAPTER THIRTEEN

Cleveland

The Terminal Tower in downtown Cleveland is nearly as large as Grand Central Station in Manhattan. I told the cab driver to take me to 2348 East 24th Street. I was on my way to see my mother. The last time I had seen her, I was in the death cells. It had been thirteen years or more.

The house was a duplex. I knocked and rang the bell so long and hard, the woman next door came out. I had begun to panic.

"Does Ida Norris live here?" I asked her.

"Yes, but she is at work now," the woman said.

"I am her son," I said.

"Come on in," the woman said, "she should be home any minute." I went into the woman's house and sat down. She told me that my mother had talked to her about me. A few minutes passed before my mother put the key in her door. The lady called to her, "Ida, come in here, I've got a surprise for you." She came in, saw me, leaped on me, hugged me and kissed me. We both were crying, tears falling everywhere.

I moved in with my mother. I explained to her how I felt I couldn't survive on parole in Alabama. I took my brother's identity and changed my name from Clarence to Willie Norris. I used Willie's name and birth certificate to get a social security card and new credentials. I found a job working for Pharoah's Machinery.

It was good to be in the bosom of my family again. Two of my sisters lived in Cleveland, Virginia and Ebeneezer. I had nieces and nephews too. I enjoyed visiting back and forth, taking the kids to the movies, buying them sweets and giving them money. They loved me.

It was a lot different living in the North. I could go anywhere I wanted and do anything without all the Jim Crow rules. I saw black and white men and women walking down the streets arm in arm. It was a strange sight to see. I took my first paycheck and went to a whorehouse. I wanted to see what all the mystery was concerning white pussy. The madam asked me what type of woman I wanted. I told her a pretty white girl would do fine. Of course all I found out was that women are alike in the sex department. Ain't no difference.

I stayed at my mother's house until the FBI came looking for me. My sister Inez was up from Tennessee visiting and staying with us. When the doorbell rang her husband answered it. It was in the evening and I was stretched out on the couch, half asleep. They walked into the house and flashed their badges.

"Does Ida Norris live here?"

"Yes," Inez said, "that's my mother." Her voice was shaking. I laid there pretending to be asleep, praying.

"Is your mother home?"

"She's upstairs in her bedroom," Inez told them.

"Do you have any brothers?"

"I have three, Willie, Clarence and Port."

"Who are these men here?" the cops asked.

"That's my brother Willie on the couch and this is my husband." One of the detectives came and stood over me. "OK, fella, wake up, let's see your identification." I got up and gave him my papers out of my wallet. The other one checked out my brother-in-law's ID.

"What's your name?" I was asked.

I said, "My name is Willie Norris."

"When is the last time you saw Clarence?" I told them I hadn't seen him since we were boys. They wanted to see my mother, so I took them upstairs.

"Mrs. Norris, have you seen or heard from your son Clarence recently?" one guy asked her.

My mother said, "No, sir, I have not heard from Clarence in many years. The last I knew anything he was in trouble in Alabama." They explained to her, how I had broken my parole. They gave her their cards and told my mother to let them know if I got in touch with her. She said she would be sure to do that, and they left. My mother didn't drink but she kept liquor for company. She kept it locked up because she didn't want her children and grandchildren to drink. That night we all got loaded.

The next day was a Sunday and I went to a movie. They were gangster pictures. I enjoyed them so much, I saw them twice. When I got home my mother was crying and hysterical. She said the detectives had come again and wanted to take me in. They had surrounded the house. They accused her of covering up for me and threatened her with jail. She had told them, "Clarence

Norris is my son, I haven't seen him and I don't know where he is, but he is long gone." They left after searching the house and questioning the neighbors.

I moved to a boardinghouse that same night. I still visited my mother when I got ready and often I'd spend two or three nights with her. She always knew where I lived and worked, so she could get ahold of me at all times.

My mother worked for a hotel in downtown Cleveland. She introduced me to a girl who worked with her. Her name was Gloria and she was a nice, good-looking woman. She and I shacked up together for about a year. We got along fine until I found out she was having affairs with other men. I caught her in several different lies and told her I had had enough. She didn't believe I would leave her.

On my way to work one day I saw a ROOM FOR RENT sign on a house. I told the woman who answered the doorbell I was interested in the room. It was a nice, clean place, so I paid her and moved in a couple of days later. My landlady's name was Mary Pierceson. She and I became very close. She had been married twice and widowed twice. She owned the house we lived in and two apartment buildings. She was an attractive lady but she was ten or twelve years older than me. We had a lot of confidence in each other though. She was good to me but I didn't love her. We had been downtown shopping and we were on the bus going home. She whispered in my ear, "Let's get married." I couldn't believe it. I explained to her how trouble had separated me and my first wife and I had promised myself never to marry again. I didn't want to give Mary up but I hadn't thought of marrying her. But I figured I had nothing to lose, since we were already living together and getting along fine. We were married before a justice of the peace.

As I have said, I loved to gamble and Cleveland was a gambler's town. Numbers and cards. My game was Georgia skin. It's a simple game. A player picks a card and the dealer shuffles off the deck. If your card comes up, you lose. Meanwhile the players can bet on whether your card will be turned up before the next man's. I was in the habit of gambling all night long, two or three days on the weekend. It was what I did to relax and enjoy myself, a hobby I picked up in the penitentiary.

Mary never said much about my gambling before we were married. But afterwards she nagged me about it all the time. She accused me of fooling around with younger women. We began to argue whenever I stayed out late. She wanted me to stop gambling altogether. I would not go for it, and things between us went from bad to worse. She changed into a crazy person. I packed up and left several times but she would beg me to come back. If she didn't know where I was living she'd send cab drivers around looking for me in places she knew I hung out. Then she'd come there, plead with me, cry and promise never to fight with me again. I'd go back to her and in a few weeks the same shit would happen again. She told me when she felt I was truly hers, she'd have all her money and deeds put in my name. I didn't marry her for that. I married her because I liked her and she loved me so much, I thought. She had been a wonderful woman, good and kind to me. Eventually I couldn't stand for her to touch me. My heart wasn't in it.

One night I was out late and I came in and gave her some money. Mary took it and threw it across the room.

I just couldn't take any more. I packed my stuff and told her there was no use coming after me because that was the end of it. I rented a kitchenette on Central Avenue and never laid eyes on the woman again.

I worked for Pharoah's Machinery for almost three years. I worked the evening shift from four to twelve. I got sort of tight with a white guy that worked there too. We'd get off work, stop for a few drinks and talk. One night he told me when he lived in California he dated a beautiful colored woman. He said she was a school-teacher and he fell in love with her. I didn't say anything, it was immaterial to me, furthermore I don't like to discuss this type of thing with a white man. A few nights later he said to me, "Willie, when are you going to invite me up to your place?" I said any time and gave him my address. Grinning, he asked me, "Are you going to have me a girl there?" I said, "I don't know about all that." He kept on, "Don't you know where I can find me a girl?" I said, "There are plenty of girls around." He said to me, "Find me a nice colored girl and I will come by your house." I told him, "When you come bring me a hot white girl and we can really have some fun." He laughed this off.

He avoided me for a while, then finally he said to me, "You know, Willie, the races shouldn't mix. White men should stick with their women and colored men with colored women. That's the way it should be." I said, "You are talking a different language than you were last week. What about that pretty schoolteacher in California?" That son of a bitch walked away from me and we never left the job together again.

I was fired off this job. I worked in the furnace department where they baked coal to make steel. I shoveled the coal out of the ovens. I put the coal on a moving belt to send it to these women to sort. They were all white women, making a good piece of money too. Sometimes their work would pile up on them and they would really have to hustle to catch up. When my work slowed down, I could relax until more coal baked. A new foreman was hired, he was from the South with that twang in his speech. Wasn't no love lost between us from the first time I saw him. He saw me sitting down one day when the women had gotten behind in their work. He told me to help them. I told him that wasn't my job. He reported me to the superintendent and he was told my job was to shovel coal and nothing else. The foreman came back and begged my pardon, but I could tell he didn't like it one bit. A week later, it was quitting time, I had cleaned my work area and I was waiting to punch out. Some guys were sweeping sand off the floor, which was what they were hired to do. The foreman came up to me: "Hey, get over there and help those guys." He had a nasty attitude. I told him I wasn't going to help them do a damn thing. He said, "Nigger, don't fool with me, I'll send you to the office." I picked up a shovel and chased him into the superintendent's office because that's where he was headed. After we told our stories, I was told to pick up my time. I was mad as hell to lose my job. I stood outside for hours waiting for that cracker, but he must have gone out another exit. He was smart because I was surely going to kick his ass.

I wasn't in a hurry to find another job. I had saved some money, so I relaxed, slept all day, gambled all night and partied. When I got tired of that I looked for work. I went to work for the National Smelting Company. I stayed there for a few months but I was laid off—the work was unsteady.

I was in a gambling joint one morning and a fella was reading the newspaper. I saw 865 and 568 in the headlines. I said, "One of those will be the number today." I played 865 and 568 for six dollars each. Then I went home and got in the bed. That evening 865 came out. I went to the numbers joint to collect my money. It was too early for me to get paid but the woman said the bookie would be there soon. I went outside and a bunch of my gambling companions were there. They started patting me on the back, telling me what a lucky guy I was and begging. I eased off from them and went back to the numbers place. I told the woman not to tell anybody I was there. Some fellas came to the door: "Willie here?" The woman said, "No the man didn't get here with the money yet and Willie said he'd be back later." No sooner than they left, the man came with the money. Three thousand dollars! I went out the back door, through a parking lot and ended up on the next street. I gave the fellas the slip.

I went to my mother's house and gave her some money but I told her I had done some carpentry work. She never would accept gambling money from me. She called it dirty money. I decided to move to New York City. My mother had lived there for years while she worked with the Communist Party, trying to get me out of the penitentiary. I was curious about such a large city. I wanted to see how I would make out in the Big Apple.

CHAPTER FOURTEEN

The Big Apple

The national office of the NAACP was my destination the second time I arrived in New York City. It was 1953 and Roy Wilkins was the administrator. He called the Young Men's Christian Association on 135th Street in Harlem and reserved a room for me. The Y was a clean, decent residence. They had all kinds of recreation there. The membership was two dollars a year and entitled you to use the swimming pool, steam bath and gym. A cafeteria was available for meals. My rent was twelve dollars a week and included maid service. There was one rule hard to get used to. Women weren't allowed in the rooms; they couldn't go farther than the lobby, which was inconvenient at times.

Strolling around town one afternoon I lost my way in the area I now know as Spanish Harlem. I asked directions from black people but they weren't speaking English. I didn't know what the hell was going on because I had never heard the language before. They were talking this funny stuff and I couldn't understand a word. I thought they were putting on airs. I got mad and cussed a couple of men out. They just kept waving their arms around and spouting these strange noises. A "brother" seeing the predicament I was in pulled my coat. I die laughing whenever I think about it. But that's how ignorant I was. I found the city to be a wild country.

I went through every damn thing as far as jobs were concerned. I went for interviews and told them what I could do, but I wasn't well received most places. The personnel people would have to fill out my application blank and that was one strike against me. No sooner than I walked out the door, my blank would be in the wastebasket. I'd be told nobody was needed, and at the same time they'd be hiring people. I worked in sweatshops so-called and they made your ass rain sweat too. Wouldn't nobody white have these jobs except the bosses. All the workers were black and Spanish. The bosses played the blacks against the Spanish. They hired Spanish people for less money because they were ignorant of the rules and hungry for work. If I wasn't careful a Puerto Rican would have my damn job. I have caught hell on most of my jobs, doing man-killing labor. Loading and unloading trucks, crating and uncrating merchandise, stacking and unstacking heavy boxes, hauling fifty-pound sacks, pushing, pulling and lifting for less than nothing in salaries. The shame of it is the hardest work pays the least. But without an education, I had to take what I could get. I have been told I needed a high school education to empty garbage cans.

Sometime in 1956 I went to Brooklyn to visit Samuel S. Leibowitz. The Scottsboro lawyer was a New York

Supreme Court judge. He held the position for thirty years. His reputation was that of a tough customer. I had heard he was giving the electric chair and long, long prison terms to most everyone who came before him and was found guilty. I peeped into his courtroom and waited for him to adjourn for the day. I went to Leibowitz's chambers and told one of his secretaries I wanted to speak with the judge. She relayed the message and two plainclothesmen came out and wanted to know why I was there. I told them my name was Clarence Norris and the judge had done some work for me in the South years ago. One cop stayed with me while the other went to report to Leibowitz. He came out a few minutes later and just stood there staring at me for some time. He grabbed my hand and shouted, "I'll be damned, it's Clarence." We went into his chambers and talked for hours.

I told him I believed in capital punishment, used correctly. I can't see a thing wrong with it, if the person is guilty of a crime that merits the supreme penalty. But when whites deserve it, they should be executed just as the blacks are. In my time the system was lopsided. During the five years I was on death row, only one white guy went to the electric chair. It was the Depression, times were hard and the whites were doing a lot of killing and stealing. When I was in the penitentiary I saw admitted white murderers serve less time than me and be released free as birds. Leibowitz and I talked about the South, the case and the law in general. He once sentenced a seventy-year-old man to twenty years. The man said, "Judge, I'll never make twenty years." Leibowitz told him, "Do the best you can." In my opinion he was right about this. Aged seventeen to seventy, if a citizen is

217

responsible for a crime they should have to pay the consequences.

He asked me how I was making it. I was out of work at the time and searching for a job. He called a few places for me but I wasn't qualified for the work. He could have gotten me a job as a chauffeur and I was sick I didn't have a driver's license. He sent me to the union that handled the city cafeterias. They got me a job on South Street, down near the docks.

I worked as a dishwasher, the pay was decent and I made a lot of overtime because the cafeteria was in a newspaper publisher's building. They were open every day of the year. I was on the job five months before I was laid off, why I don't know.

I never saw Leibowitz again except on television. He was asked if he knew where any of the Scottsboro Boys were, and he said he had seen one of us in the garment district. I don't know who that could have been.

Over the years I have worked on a string of different jobs. I've worked for businesses all over the city, in Harlem, Brooklyn and Queens. I've held jobs in Yonkers, upstate New York and in New Jersey. A job I really enjoyed was baking cakes and pies in a Harlem restaurant. It was a side gig, only part-time, but it was fun. I fell out with the owner though and had to quit.

At 10 Sanford Street in Brooklyn I made pipe fittings. I was injured one afternoon when a hand truck I was pushing slipped and hit me in the groin. That night I couldn't sleep because of the pain. I went to Harlem Hospital's emergency room and I swear the place was a slaughter pen. There were about twenty-five people in there waiting to see doctors. Some were cut or shot.

The Big Apple

Blood was everywhere and the moaning and groaning was awful. The doctors and nurses were walking around laughing and talking as if the patients weren't there. A woman came in whose head was split open; she sat and nobody did a thing for her.

I got the hell out of there and caught a taxi to Metropolitan Hospital. I was treated right away and given something for the pain. Afterwards I was treated by a private doctor for six weeks. I finally got myself straightened out, and since I was hurt on the job I got a little piece of money. This company moved to Florida and didn't pay the workers severance pay or vacation time. They just took off; one day they were there and the next they were gone. They had asked us to invest in the business months before, so most of us had given a percentage of our paychecks weekly, hoping to reap promised dividends. It turned out we had been giving our money away.

My new job was with Lawrence Plastics Company on 20th Street, between Park and Fifth Avenue in Manhattan. I was there for three and a half years. I sprained my shoulder muscles loading a truck with boxes of this plastic. I couldn't lift my arms and I was out of work for two months. The company went out of business and I didn't know what to do. I went to the International Labor Defense to get a lawyer. I was shocked to see Allan Taub there. The same lawyer who came with Joe Brodsky and sneaked into the jail at Gadsden in 1931. He was overjoyed at seeing me. He got $2,848.20 from the insurance company of Lawrence Plastics for me and didn't charge me but a hundred dollars.

We went all over town together and he wanted to

write my life story but I told him I couldn't stand the publicity. I wasn't taking the chance of going back to the penitentiary on anybody's say-so. Taub introduced me to a man who became a good friend. I went to a party at this man's house one night, and that is where I met my third wife, Melva. She was a lovely young woman with a two-year-old daughter named Bernadine. We were married in 1960 and we have been together ever since. We have two teenage daughters of our own, Adele and Deborah. Deborah is nineteen and has a two-year-old child; she's the most beautiful grandbaby a man could have. Adele is sixteen and still in high school.

I helped to raise Bernadine as my own and we tried to give her all we could, and so did her grandparents. I have no use for Bernadine today. She finished junior high school but she didn't spend a day in senior high. She became a heroin user—shooting it in her veins. She was fooling with a twenty-year-old man and she wouldn't go to school any more. She refused to listen to all of us that tried to help her. The boy is dead now from an overdose. He wanted to marry Bernadine. She was too young, and she had terrible fights with Melva because she wouldn't sign the papers for Bernadine to marry another dope addict. It was a sin and a shame what that girl put us through. We finally had to put her out because she was stealing us blind, and I didn't want her around my kids with that poison. An addict will kill you to get what they need. Bernadine has two children; my wife and I take care of them. Her son and daughter live with us. She is twenty years old now and still a junkie.

I moved my family to Brooklyn to get them out of Harlem. We live in the public housing on Linden Boule-

vard. The neighborhood is mostly private homes and it's
quiet out there. The schools are probably better too.

New York City is a tough city to survive in. I started
carrying a gun after I was robbed. It happened twenty
years ago. I had left a bar on 124th and Lenox Avenue,
the Sports Inn. They followed me out of there. I had
been gambling and I had three hundred and eighty dollars on me. I was hit in the head and I fell to the
sidewalk. I was beaten and kicked in the face. Some of
my teeth were knocked out and broken off. The three of
them went through my pockets and took my money,
then they ran away. It happened as fast as lightning. A
fellow came over to help me. He asked if I was all right
and led me to a bathroom in a building a couple of doors
away. He told me I could wash up in there. I went in
and shut the door. I was in there a while trying to get
myself together. I was dizzy and nauseous. The guy was
in the hall, he called out, "Need any help?" I came out
and there were four niggers waiting with knives. The one
who had helped me said, "Go up those stairs, all the way
to the roof." I said, "Man, I ain't got no more money,
you saw me get robbed." He hit me on the head with a
wine bottle and told me to "move it." Blood was running
down my face and neck. On the roof they made me take
off every piece of clothing, shoes, socks, everything. I had
some change and they took that. They went through
every pocket, cuff and seam of those clothes. I was laying
on my stomach, naked on the goddamn roof. They discussed what to do with me and decided to let me go. One
guy bent over me and said, "You're going to forget you
ever saw us, aren't you?" I said, "Man, I ain't never seen
you." He told me to put my clothes on, go down the

steps and not to turn towards the police station. I walked over to 125th Street, I was bleeding like a pig. I saw two cops and told them what had happened to me. They asked me if I knew the guys. I told them no, but I'd recognize them if I ever saw them again. The policemen did not move from the spot; one told me I had better get to a hospital. I went to the police station and reported the crime. They didn't even ask for a description of the thieves. They just told me I'd better get medical treatment, but no one offered to take me there. They didn't give a damn about none of it.

I walked over to Harlem Hospital; two hours later I was treated by a doctor and taken to X-ray. I didn't have any broken bones or a skull fracture, so they sent me home.

I was in a rage at how defenseless I was and how unconcerned the cops were. Survival is important to me and I refused to be prey for the thieving bastards in this city. I bought me a gun and when I have to be in the streets late at night, it goes with me. I have been caught with it several times, arrested and fined up to two hundred dollars. But I would rather pay the money or go to jail than lose my life.

The first time I was arrested for possession of a gun, I was in an after-hours spot. The police broke into the place and lined us up against the wall. We were searched and they found my gun. I was taken to jail with the guys who owned the place. I was fingerprinted before I was put in a cell in the Tombs and again before I went to court the next day. I was fined two hundred dollars and released.

Another time a girlfriend and I were running a gambling game and we were set up by an undercover police-man. I pleaded guilty and the judge put me on probation for two years.

Four years later I was arrested for stabbing my woman, Liz. We were drinking and got into an argument. We ran a gambling house. Earlier that night I took a knife away from a guy who threatened to cut his wife. I had it in my pocket when Liz and I began fighting. She shoved a chair between my legs, and before I thought about it, I had stabbed her in the throat. The knife went into her neck all the way up to the handle. The house was full of people and somebody called the police. By the time they came nobody was there except me and Liz. I didn't try to run away. An ambulance came for Liz and the police took me to the Tombs. Liz and I were lucky, she survived. She wouldn't sign the complaint against me, so the charges were dropped. I had to go before the judge though and he told me he never wanted to see my face in his courtroom again.

The last time I was arrested was in the summer of 1976. I was home with my wife and children. I was laying across the bed in my room when I heard loud noises at the door. Two boys were banging on the door with a stick. They were looking for a friend of my daughter's, another teenaged girl. Adele opened the door, and the boys jumped her. One of them had a stick and the other one had a knife. Melva was screaming at the top of her lungs. I jumped up and grabbed my gun out of the dresser. The boys had run out of the apartment but I found them sitting on the steps near the elevator. I asked them what they had been trying to do. One of them stood up and pulled a knife on me. He said, "I don't know what you have in your pocket, but if you bring it out I'll make you eat it." I hollered at him, "Eat some of these .38's." I emptied the gun at the kid. I didn't shoot to kill but I scared the shit out of him. I thought he would kill himself running up the stairs. I went back to my apartment and put the gun in the dresser.

Somebody called the police and in the next few minutes they had surrounded the building. We live on the sixth floor and I thought to throw the gun out of the window but I didn't want it on my conscience if it got into the wrong hands. Six cops barged in with drawn guns and demanded the pistol. At first I denied I had one. They said, "We'll tear the place apart till we find it, so you might as well hand it over." I wasn't allowed to get it myself, I had to tell them where it was. I explained what had happened with the teenagers. They said they understood me protecting my home but they would have to take me in. I was fingerprinted and had mug shots taken at the Tombs. I had to go to court several times and I pleaded self-defense. I was finally charged with not having a permit for the gun and fined two hundred dollars. The housing authority tried to evict me from my apartment but the NAACP helped me fight them. A hearing was held and they dropped the eviction attempt.

Over the years I have been arrested and fingerprinted so many times I have lost count. It happened in Cleveland as well as in New York. I would get rounded up in gambling raids most of the time. While the police had me locked up I would be nervous they might be able to trace me back to Alabama. Why they didn't or couldn't I don't know. But there are people the law just don't catch because the system fails a lot of the time. They make mistakes.

The Big Apple

Clarence Crenshaw was a convicted murderer who killed a white man. He was in the death cells with me when he got a new trial and was sentenced to life. He escaped from a prison road gang. I ran into him sitting on a shoe shine stand in Harlem. He wanted to write a book about the Alabama prisons but I told him no because we both might have ended up back there. I haven't seen him since and that was years ago.

I have met up with quite a few guys I knew in prison who had long sentences and escaped. I was friendly with two in Cleveland. Gene Foster who I saw in Cleveland, then met again years later in New York, had murdered a black man. He was living on St. Nicholas Avenue with a wife and three children. He was caught in Delaware for speeding. He was fingerprinted but they let him go after he paid his fine. A week later the police came to his house and arrested him. They tracked him to New York through his driver's license. He fought extradition and now he is free.

Andy Wright and Olen Montgomery are the only Scottsboro Boys I've seen since I left Alabama. Willie Roberson lived in Brooklyn, but when Olen took me to see him one Saturday the people at the house said he had died the week before. I was all prepared to see Willie and it shocked me to learn he was dead. He had an asthma attack and choked to death.

Roy Wright lived in Harlem, but I never got to see him before he committed suicide. His job with the Merchant Marine kept him out of town quite a bit. Andy was living in Connecticut but he'd come to New York and we'd get together. But I never saw him after his brother killed himself. Olen Montgomery went back South to live and I don't know if he's dead or alive.

225

Word got around over the years that I was one of the Scottsboro Boys. Everywhere I turned somebody wanted to write a book or an article about my life. Of course they didn't know I was still wanted by Alabama. If they did they didn't care and just wanted to make a name for themselves and some money. I always refused to be interviewed by any writers or reporters.

There was a gentleman named Henry Moon who worked for the NAACP, and he was a friend of mine. He called me one day and said some woman wanted to write an article for *FACT* magazine about the case. She had written a book on the three civil rights workers who were killed in Mississippi, lynched by those crackers during the freedom rides in the sixties. I made an appointment to see her. I told her if I gave her magazine any information about my case, I would be wanting some money. She said she was authorized to give me a hundred dollars. I gave her a hundred dollars worth of information. She would have learned more at the library. She wanted to see me again and invited me to her house but I never went. I figured she wanted to write something big and it wouldn't benefit me none.

I worked for the city of New York for five years before I retired in July 1977. My title was that of warehouseman. I operated a machine like the sweepers used to clean the streets. I rode on the machine to clean and wax the floors in a city warehouse. The building was eight stories high and three blocks long. It was the best job I ever had. I got along well with my supervisors and the other workers. I was my own boss, with nobody hovering over me, telling me what to do. It is good to feel secure in a job. I am happy that my last working days were for the city I have lived in and loved all these years.

The Big Apple

Everybody is given the gift of life and wants to live that life to the fullest. When you want to live good, you think good and do good, to me that's it. Many good deeds have been done for me and I have tried to do my share of them for other people. But you can't help hurting somebody if you live long enough and I imagine I have.

The penitentiary is a hell of a place but I got a lesson from it. It taught me how to make it in the free world. I learned how to do a lot of things in prison. I don't have any schooling, but I have always wanted to do what anybody else could do. I'd like to express myself better but my wisdom won't let me. A good education is the best thing in the world to have but common sense is important too. Mother wit is what I live by. The hell away with what I have missed. There is nothing I can do about the past, so I don't worry about it any more. I'm not going to let life run me nuts.

I've made some mistakes since I've been on the free streets but so has every man. Most of the trouble I've had with the law is because I was a gambler. Gambling was a habit with me. I gambled because I was usually making just a small salary and when I hit the number for five or six hundred dollars or won a few bucks at cards it was money in the bank. Of course I lost a lot of money too, but it takes a good sport to gamble and I'm not a hard loser. As I got older I got wiser. I left the cheating alone because too many guys get killed from it. These days I'll get into a poker game every now and then but nothing heavy. Sometimes I play the numbers when I get a hunch. I don't take the chances I took when I was a younger man.

In 1970 I decided to gamble that times had changed

for the better in Alabama. I was nearing retirement age and I wanted to clear my name. My kids were growing up and they didn't even know who I was. I didn't want them to find out someday I was a convicted rapist without knowing my side of the story. I had to fight for my rights so they will have the courage to fight for theirs.

CHAPTER FIFTEEN

Vindication

I was never guilty of anything except stealing a ride on a freight train during the Depression, just as the poor whites were doing. Mean, prejudiced crackers, thinking they were better than me, decided to throw me off that train along with the other blacks. I imagine they thought it would be easy enough. They would tell us to unload and we'd go peacefully. When we didn't do their bidding, they threw rocks at us and we just didn't go for it. We threw their asses off the train in a fair fight and they went running to the nearest sheriff to report a pack of uppity niggers.

Victoria Price and Ruby Bates were riding on a different part of that train and I never saw either of them until they accused me of rape in Scottsboro. When the train was stopped at Paint Rock, I think the women were intimidated by the mob, and some of those crackers probably asked them what they were doing on that train with "all these niggers." They put the finger on us to win sympathy for themselves. Victoria Price stuck to her lie throughout the years even after Ruby Bates owned up to the true facts.

Dr. John Morsell and I were discussing all this one day in the NAACP office. [Until his death in 1975 Morsell was assistant to Roy Wilkins.] I told him I was tired of this thing hanging over my head and I wanted to make a bid for my complete freedom. We decided that after twenty-four years, the officials of Alabama would lift my parole violation. Dr. Morsell introduced me to the NAACP's chief counsel, Nathaniel Jones. Mr. Jones wrote to Fred Gray, a prominent black lawyer in Montgomery, on January 26, 1971. He wrote in part: "Our Association desires to assist Norris in having the violation lifted, if in fact he is still carried as a parole violator. He is anxious to bring this nightmare to an end. ... I realize that this is an extremely delicate situation; however, we are confident that you will know the precise moves that should be made in handling this matter."

Two and a half years passed and I didn't hear any more about it. I'd see Mr. Jones in the corridors of the NAACP offices and he would walk past me without a word. I got so disgusted, I called Alabama myself in June of 1973. I called the governor's office and asked to speak to George Wallace. The woman who answered the phone said he wasn't there. I asked to speak to somebody next to him. A man came on the line, he told me his name but it's been so long I have forgotten it. He asked how he could help me. I told him, "My name is Clarence Norris, one of the Scottsboro Boys. I was arrested in Alabama in 1931 and sentenced to the electric chair three times. The governor commuted my sentence to life in prison. I was released on parole twice, once in 1944, and I broke my

230

parole and went back to prison until I got out in 1946. I broke my parole again and I have been free ever since. I want to know if Alabama still wants me." He said that he couldn't tell me anything. He gave me the phone number of the Alabama Department of Corrections and Institutions. I called there and explained myself to the guy who answered the phone. He told me to hold on. He went somewhere, looked up the records or whatever. He came back on the line and said to me, "Yes, we want you and I will do everything in my power to get you back." I said, "Mister, I have been away from Alabama for over twenty years." He asked me for my phone number. I gave him a phony number. "What's your address?" I gave him a phony address.

I went to the NAACP office and had a conversation with Roy Wilkins. He introduced me to another of their lawyers, a young Jewish man named James Meyerson. We spent a lot of time discussing the case, and Meyerson said he would do all he could to get the show on the road.

His first step was to find out what Mr. Jones had done, then he wrote to Fred Gray. Meyerson wrote me in July of 1973: "I have not heard back from Mr. Gray regarding his efforts on your behalf, so I have written to him requesting that he get moving. If he does not do so, I think that we will have to find another attorney who is less busy and/or more concerned to deal with this matter."

In September Meyerson sent me a copy of a letter he had received from Mr. Gray. It said in part: "Please forgive my delay in responding to your letters of June 18 and July 23, 1973. I have assigned my associate, Mr. Cleveland Thorton, to look into the possibility of helping

Mr. Norris in this matter. As you suggested, we are looking into the possibility of both a pardon, or the alternative, to remove Mr. Norris' parole to New York."

December 19, 1973, Meyerson sent me a copy of a letter he wrote to Fred Gray: "I have not heard from you since your letter of September 27, 1973. I know that you are extremely busy but I was wondering if Mr. Thorton had completed his investigation and discussed the matter with you. Since this is the holiday season, I was hoping that we could have some positive news for Mr. Norris."

The New Year came and went and months rolled around. It wasn't until October 10, 1974, that Jimmy Meyerson received a letter from Donald Watkins, another associate in Fred Gray's law firm. This was after several unanswered letters and phone calls to their offices in Montgomery. Attorney Watkins explained that during the years of 1972 and 1973 their law firm was "completely inundated in trying to expose, ascertain the dimension and perimeters of and handle the Tuskegee Syphilis Study." [The case involved a number of black men known to be afflicted with syphilis who as part of a study of the disease were deliberately left untreated by white doctors.] He wrote further that Title 42, Section 18 (3) of the Alabama Code governs pardons of persons whose sentence to death has been commuted. Such persons "... shall not ... be eligible for a pardon unless sufficient evidence is presented to the Board of Pardons and Paroles to satisfy it that such person was innocent of the crime for which he was convicted and said board votes unanimously to grant such person a pardon, and the governor concurs in and approves the granting of the pardon."

Vindication

That week Donald Watkins met with Governor Wallace's legal adviser and the executive director of the pardons and paroles board. After these meetings he called Jim Meyerson and said, "A pardon is unlikely, but a transfer of parole is probable." It was explained to me that the New York state parole authorities would have to accept jurisdiction over me and a background check made to verify that I had been an upright citizen for the last twenty-eight years. I would have to return to Alabama and turn myself in to the authorities, acknowledge that I was a parole violator, and only then would Alabama release me to the custody of New York. I would also have to spend one night in jail there. The lawyers said they believed something could be worked out where I wouldn't be locked up if I went back. I told them to go to hell. The executive director of the Alabama board said there was nothing they could do for me because "technically I was a fugitive from justice."

I thought the case had reached a dead end; things had bogged down to a stalemate. Meyerson and I discussed reopening the case and the possibilities of a new trial. We knew this would result in wide-scale publicity and maybe it would help me. He felt that at my age of sixty-three there was little likelihood that even the state of Alabama would do anything to hurt me. Of course he didn't really know the first thing about Alabama, no more than Leibowitz did. I told him how Leibowitz had been threatened and called a "dirty Yankee Jew." But he told me it was a brand-new world, and I was anxious to have a new trial if that was the case.

We kicked the idea around for about a year until Jimmy read in the paper that the attorney general of Alabama, William J. Baxley, had indicted three Ku Klux

Klansmen for the murder of a black kid back in 1957. He got very excited and told me he was going to write Watkins and ask him to approach the attorney general's office in my regard. It turned out that Watkins was acquainted with an Alabama assistant attorney general, Milton C. Davis, who I was shocked to learn was a black man—and I was also pleased and proud. Donald met with Attorney Davis and outlined my case and what he had been trying to do for the past five years. Davis asked Watkins to write him a letter summarizing the case and he would take it to the attorney general. This was done. A meeting was set up between Watkins, Davis and the attorney general. The attorney general was familiar with the case, as most lawyers are. They have to study the Powell case and the Norris case in constitutional law while they are in school. Baxley agreed to take an active role in seeking a pardon for me. He assigned Mr. Davis to handle everything. Donald wrote Jimmy that the attorney general did not commit himself, but Mr. Baxley's personal view was that a pardon was the least that Alabama could do. This meeting took place in April of 1976.

On May 19, 1976, Roy Wilkins sent a letter to different officials of New York State. The letter went out to Governor Hugh Carey, Mayor Abraham D. Beame, Senator James Buckley, Senator Jacob K. Javits, Borough President of Manhattan Percy E. Sutton and Presiding Justice of the New York State Supreme Court Harold Stevens. The letter read in part: "For some time now the NAACP has been attempting to assist the lone remaining Scottsboro defendant to obtain a pardon from the Governor of Alabama. It appears that such might be possible, if, among other things, expressions of approval are received from responsible persons in New York."

234

Vindication

Percy Sutton was the first to answer the letter. He endorsed the efforts of the NAACP as did Justice Harold Stevens, Mayor Beame and Senator Javits. Governor Carey wrote in part, through his assistant counsel, Clarence Sundram: "As a chief executive who is himself called upon to exercise the power of clemency, Governor Carey is cognizant of the need for a thorough inquiry prior to deciding upon the propriety of clemency in a particular case. I realize that such an inquiry may hamper the ability to respond swiftly but it is nonetheless necessary." We didn't hear from Governor Carey again.

A letter read to me that came from Professor Dan T. Carter of Emory University in Atlanta impressed me most of all. It read in part: "There is today an organization called the 'Flat Earth Society.' Its thousands of members believe that the earth is flat and no amount of proof or persuasion can convince them otherwise. Well, I spent the better part of two years researching and writing an account of that case. I read over 10,000 pages of trial transcripts; I went over hundreds of newspaper accounts and first-hand reports. I read through the correspondence of every major organization involved in the case. Finally, I reviewed the medical testimony with several experts in the field. And I tell you flatly that I would join the Flat Earth Society before I would accept the notion that Victoria Price and Ruby Bates were raped on March 25, 1931."

I celebrated my sixty-fourth birthday with the hope that I would soon be as free as any man. On August 5, 1976, the Alabama attorney general signed the official opinion, drafted by Milton Davis, based on his findings in the case of the *State of Alabama vs. Clarence Norris.*

The opinion stated that I was innocent of the crime for which I was convicted, and it recommended that I be granted a pardon. The opinion was sent to Norman F. Ussery, the chairman of the pardons and paroles board.

Mr. Ussery replied: "It is my feeling that as long as Mr. Norris is a fugitive from justice and there is an outstanding warrant against him, it would not be proper even to consider him for a pardon at this time."

When the lawyers got this information, everybody was upset. Donald Watkins went to see Ussery, who reinforced his letter by indicating I would have to go to prison for at least three years before I could get any consideration from the board. Donald called Jim Meyerson and told him the response from the board was so negative that the situation looked hopeless. He suggested reopening the case and preparation for a new trial. Jimmy wouldn't accept this analysis. He said it was time to bring the matter to the attention of the public through the news media. He asked Donald to set up a meeting between Ussery, the Alabama attorney general and all concerned parties; he would go to Alabama when the date was set.

Jimmy sent Alabama Governor George Wallace copies of the letters that had been written to Ussery by New York officials, recommending my pardon. He conferred with Roy Wilkins, and Mr. Wilkins sent a telegram to the governor asking him to use his influence with the board. The telegram read: ". . . charity, mercy and justice, even though delayed, would be served by immediately lifting from Clarence Norris and from Alabama's judicial system the burden of making new and unnecessary assessments." Copies were sent to Ussery, the United States attorney general and William Baxley.

236

Vindication

I was interviewed by Thomas Johnson of the New York *Times* for a story that appeared on the front page of that paper on October 9, 1976. The next morning David Kladstrup of CBS came to my home with a television crew and filmed an interview that was broadcast on the evening news program. During that week editorials appeared in the Washington *Post,* the New York *Times* and the Montgomery *Advertiser* stating that I had suffered enough and it was time for Alabama to cleanse its conscience. I was interviewed by Tom Jory of the Associated Press, Andy Kilpatrick of the Birmingham *News,* Lynora Williams of the *Guardian Press,* Jack Hartsfield of the Montgomery *Advertiser* and Paul Cowan of the *Village Voice* and by people from the National Black Network, and *Jet* magazine.

Letters of support poured in from all over the country—to me, Governor Wallace and Norman Ussery. Colonel Joe Burleson, who was in charge of the National Guard during the trials at Decatur in 1933, wrote Ussery and Baxley: "... after hearing the evidence I was convinced at that time, and I am still convinced, that Clarence Norris and all the other co-defendants in that case were completely innocent. I have often hoped that the opportunity to help these men would come my way. ..."

My NAACP lawyer went to Alabama, October 13, 1976. He met with Baxley, Watkins, Davis and Ussery. Ussery told him that it was impossible to pardon me legally while I was still a fugitive. He said I would have to surrender to Alabama authorities; a hearing would be set up, and possibly I would be reinstated on parole, and after I served the required successful three years on parole, they would consider a pardon. I had no intention of surrendering to anybody!

Milton Davis explained to Ussery that any state official who acts in accordance with an attorney general's opinion on a legal issue, that official is insulated from any liability. That is an Alabama state statute and that is why attorney generals' opinions are sought. When Ussery realized he didn't have a legal front to try and force me to surrender in order to get the pardon, he said it wasn't necessary but it would be "the right thing to do."

By now the reporters were calling everyone involved in the case from Governor Wallace to me. I couldn't sleep for the reporters calling me and the lawyers calling me to ask what I would do in the event of this or that. I told them I wasn't going back to Alabama without my pardon in my hand. At the meeting with the attorneys and Ussery they tried to get in there with television cameras but that was vetoed. So the newsmen talked to them when they came out of the meeting. I was looking at them on the TV and listening to them on the radio. The press wanted to know when, if ever, there was going to be a development in the case. The people on my job were driving me crazy too, so I took some of my vacation days and went to stay with a friend in Harlem. I didn't want to be at home or at work because I didn't know what might happen now that everybody knew where I was.

Donald Watkins and Milton Davis met with Ussery at his request the next morning. He said he might be able to arrange for me to surrender to them, instead of law enforcement officials, then it would not be necessary to handcuff me.

After these meetings the pressure of adverse public opinion was brought to bear on the governor's office and the pardons and paroles board. The attorney general had

238

stated to the board, in writing, on two separate occasions that after a review of all the evidence, which he also submitted to the board, I was innocent of the crime for which I had been convicted. And according to the Alabama Code I was due a pardon. So what was the holdup? I didn't understand it.

There were three members of the pardons and paroles board but the lawyers had never talked to any of them except Norman Ussery, because he was the chairman. It was assumed the other two members, Mrs. Sara Cousins Sellers and William R. Robinson, were in agreement with Ussery, but that was not the case. Mrs. Sellers and Mr. Robinson issued a statement and wrote me a letter that they had voted to withdraw the warrant for my arrest and void my parole delinquency. I was no longer a fugitive.

That day Norman Ussery went to the governor's office to discuss the situation. Under Alabama law the governor does not have the right to pardon. After the unanimous decision of the parole board to pardon somebody, the governor can either approve or veto it. Ussery told my lawyers and the attorney general's office that each of them had to submit a written statement of reasons for the board to adopt, in the case the pardon was granted. The law that applied to me states I had to prove to the board that I was innocent of the crime and they had to agree unanimously that I was.

On October 25, 1976, the attorney general gave the board his official findings of fact. The members wrote on that document they were adopting it as proof that I was innocent, and they signed it. The certificate of pardon which restored my civil and political rights was signed by them and taken over to Governor Wallace, who signed it, and from that point on I was a free man. Jim Meyerson was in Alabama and he called me the night before and told me the pardon would be approved. I found it hard to believe, but it happened.

There were press releases by the governor's office, Ussery and the NAACP. That afternoon I was in my regular hangout in Harlem when people started coming in telling me I was free. When people found out I was in there, the place filled up. By the time the woman who is writing this book with me called me there, I was feeling no pain. She told me the NAACP offices were swamped with reporters and television crews; they wanted me down there.

The first thing they wanted to know was if I was going to sue Alabama. How did I feel? What was I doing when I heard the good news? What were my plans? It had been thirty years and one month since I had left Alabama. It had been forty-five years of being hounded for something I didn't do. I was full and I couldn't hold the tears back. I was thinking of those other eight boys who grew to manhood in the penitentiary.

Alabama Revisited—
Epilogue

The day they notified me I would receive my pardon, my sister called the NAACP office and left a message for me to get in touch with her. My sister Virginia, who lives in Cleveland. It was the first time I had heard from any of my relatives in twenty-three years. This was one of the main reasons I wanted the pardon so bad, because I wanted to see my brothers, sisters, nieces and nephews before it was too late for me. As soon as the press conference was over, Meyerson gave me the message and I called Virginia. It was the greatest thrill of my life but I cried like a baby when she told me my mother had passed away the year before. She put her daughter, Inez, on the phone; the last time I had seen her she was a toddler, and now she had teenagers of her own. I was beside myself with joy and sadness. My oldest sister, Lucille, had passed away too, but all the others were alive and healthy. I couldn't wait to see them all and I had lots of nieces and nephews I had never seen before. Now that I was free I could visit Blanche and Willie in Georgia, Port in Florida and Virginia, Ebeneezer, Ina Mae and Inez in Cleveland. This had been my dream.

The NAACP asked me if I would go on a speaking tour to help raise money for the organization. I was more than happy to do this for them after all they had done for me. The first stop on the itinerary was happily Cleveland. Then Baltimore, Montgomery, Tuscaloosa, Pensacola, St. Petersburg, Orlando, Miami, Los Angeles, San Francisco and Seattle. I took four weeks' leave of absence from my job to do this.

The people came out to see me in droves in most places, and they made me feel so welcome that I never experienced any nervousness in speaking to them. I told them what had happened to me in 1931 and since and I explained to them the help that the NAACP had given me. I told them the organization was valuable to black people in every respect and it is the only organization that we could go to for help when we were in deep trouble. It was fun to me, meeting all the people that wanted to shake my hand and signing autographs like a big movie star or somebody. Plus I was flying around on the airplanes which I had never done before and going places I had never seen or thought I would, so it was an exciting time for me. If there was a place I wanted to live besides New York City, it would be San Francisco, that's a pretty town.

I never thought I'd see the day that I would go back to Alabama for any reason whatsoever. And as far as I was concerned I could have skipped that, and they could have mailed the pardon to me. But plans were made for the pardons and paroles board to give me the pardon personally in the Capitol building in Montgomery.

On November 29, 1976, I returned to Alabama a free man, nearly forty-six years after being taken off that freight train. There were a few hundred people waiting at the airport, and to be frank I was scared to get off the plane. I thought there might be some crazy cracker in the crowd who would take a shot at me. But Meyerson convinced me they were all well-wishers out there. I didn't believe that, but when he told me security had been arranged for, I got out of the airplane. The people were pushing and shoving, the reporters were there and the TV cameras, men were shaking my hand and women were kissing on me. I was rushed to a car. It was all a blur, although I know I was answering questions and everything. I was in a daze. I'd never seen the like and I couldn't believe it was happening in Alabama. We got to the Capitol building about eleven o'clock that morning, and there was a mob there too. Everybody was smiling and telling me how happy they were that I was free. The reporters kept asking me how it felt to be free.

We all packed into the pardons and paroles board's office, and Norman Ussery made a little speech of welcome. He shook my hand and gave me the pardon. The other board members congratulated me and wished me well. Lots of pictures were being taken. As we walked down the hall and out of the building a man walked up to me and asked me if I remembered him. His name was Luther Birchfield, and he had been a prisoner in Kilby at the same time as me. We called him "Railhead." It was good to see him out alive and well.

We left there and went directly to the Dexter Avenue

Baptist Church for a press conference. The same church where Martin Luther King, Jr., started the civil rights movement. The church was full with wall-to-wall people, black and white. Roy Wilkins made a speech and several others who were involved in the case. I told the reporters I was glad to be free, that I had no hard feelings against Alabama and that the past was buried as far as my concern. I said I wanted my pardon because it was due me and because of my kids, my family. I expressed my feeling that the thing I wished for more than anything in the world was for Haywood, Ozie, Andy, Roy, Olen, Eugene, Willie and Charlie to be there with me, and that they deserved the same pardon as myself.

Attorney General William Baxley took me and the rest of my group to lunch at a big, fancy restaurant. This is the man that I knew was really responsible for me receiving the pardon. Alabama had surely changed, we all sat together at a large table. The attorney general and his wife, Mr. and Mrs. Roy Wilkins, Vanzetta Durant, a black woman assistant attorney general, Rufus Huffman, a black probate judge, Alvin Holmes, a black member of the State House of Representatives, Ruby Hurley, the southeast regional director of the NAACP, James Meyerson, Donald Watkins, Sybil Washington, Nathaniel Jones and Fred Gray. I was sitting at the head of the table, but I couldn't believe I was in Alabama.

That evening there was a rally for the NAACP at Reverend J. T. Hemphill's church on Jeff Davis Avenue. It was the largest church I'd ever been in and it was beautiful too. People were standing because they couldn't get a seat and everybody must have had a camera, including the TV cameramen. Those guys came in and set up their lights and machinery just like nobody

was there. They had several choirs from around the city
... they sang their hearts out. Everybody involved in
getting the pardon gave a speech to much clapping and
cheering, and a fine time was had by all.

A beautiful, older black woman gave me a cross on a
chain after the ceremonies. She said she made it especially for me. It is a heavy silver cross, three inches
long and two inches wide, wonderfully carved with circu-
lar designs. The gift really touched my heart. The lady
said she had been praying for me to be free of my troubles. I wish I knew her name; she was a complete
stranger and I'll never forget her. I wear the cross and I
think of her often.

The people I had come with from New York and the
others I met since getting to Alabama came back to my
hotel room. We got there in time to see ourselves on
television. The attorney general had given me copies of
my pardon that I autographed on request and passed
around. We had drinks and sent out for chicken and
traded tales. Around twelve o'clock Alvin Holmes called
Governor Wallace and handed me the phone. He said
he'd like to see me before I went home. You could have
knocked me over with a feather. I had a hard time getting to sleep that night, I had had a day to be cherished
in memory. It was a brand-new world for me.

The next morning I went to Tuscaloosa, where I made
a speech at the University of Alabama. The school where
Wallace had stood in the door to keep blacks out. It was
wonderful to see the black and white students walking,
talking and sitting together. I stayed in Tuscaloosa most
of the day and it seemed like I shook hands with a
thousand people.

The next morning I was ushered into the governor's

office along with Sybil Washington, Alvin Holmes, James Meyerson, Donald Watkins, Fred Gray and Rufus Huffman. He was sitting behind the biggest desk you can imagine. He had a chair sitting beside his and he asked me to sit there. He grabbed my hand and just held it for a while. He told me he was happy to have been the one to sign my pardon. He said he had been a small boy when my trouble started in 1931 and that he had been in the service when I was on parole in 1944. He said relationships were good between blacks and whites in Alabama now and they had come a long way. "We are not a utopia," the governor said, "we've got a long way to go as does every place else, but we don't have to go as far as most places ... I'm glad for it and praise the Lord for it, frankly." He told me I was looking good and prosperous, and I said I had been working and taking care of myself. He asked my age, and when I told him I was sixty-four wanted to know how black people stay young-looking for so long. Alvin Holmes told the governor, "That's because we eat a lot of soul food, fried chicken, collard greens and you whites eat a lot of steaks." The governor replied, "I like collards as well as you do. I used to eat cold coon and collards for breakfast." The meeting lasted about thirty minutes. Wallace invited me to come back and see him any time I was in Montgomery, and we wished each other long lives.

We left and went and had lunch at the University of Alabama in Montgomery where Donald Watkins introduced me to his father who is the president of the university. Then Jimmy Meyerson and me took a plane to Pensacola, where I was to speak the next day.

I had spent years in Alabama and I had been treated

246

worse than a dog, treated as nothing. The world changed and in the three days I was in Alabama, during that time, I was treated as a king and to me that is what every free man is!

Chronological Record of the Scottsboro Case

MARCH 25:   Clarence Norris, Olen Montgomery, Ozie Powell, Haywood Patterson, Willie Roberson, Charlie Weems, Eugene Williams, Roy and Andy Wright—nine black youths—are taken off a freight train at Paint Rock, Alabama, by a mob. They are brought to the nearest jail, in Scottsboro, Alabama.

MARCH 26:   All nine are charged with the rape of two white women, Victoria Price and Ruby Bates. The prisoners are moved to Gadsden, Alabama, by the National Guard to insure their safety.

APRIL 9:   Judge Alfred E. Hawkins sentences all but thirteen-year-old Roy Wright to die by electrocution on July 10, 1931.

APRIL 25:   The International Labor Defense, a Communist organization, launches a worldwide protest, as thousands march in Harlem to free the Scottsboro Boys.

MAY 3: The National Association for the Advancement of Colored People enters the case when Walter White, the executive director of the NAACP, visits Kilby prison in Montgomery to see the Scottsboro Boys.

JUNE 22: Execution date is set aside pending appeal to higher courts.

1932

NOVEMBER 7: The United States Supreme Court orders new trials for the defendants, on the grounds that they did not receive adequate counsel at Scottsboro in violation of their civil rights under the fourteenth amendment to the Constitution.

1933

MARCH 6: The new trials are scheduled to be held in Decatur, Morgan County, after Judge Hawkins grants a change of venue.

MARCH 13: William L. Patterson, executive director of the International Labor Defense, retains Samuel S. Leibowitz, a famed New York criminal lawyer, for the defense.

MARCH 27: Haywood Patterson is the first to be tried; Judge James E. Horton presides.

APRIL 7: Ruby Bates takes the witness stand and denies she or Victoria Price was raped.

APRIL 9: Haywood Patterson is found guilty and sentenced to die on June 16, 1933.

JUNE 22: Judge Horton orders a new trial for Patterson on the grounds that the evidence did not warrant a conviction.

DECEMBER 6: Clarence Norris' jury finds him guilty as charged. He is scheduled to die on February 2, 1934; date suspended pending appeal.

1934

OCTOBER 1: International Labor Defense lawyers Samuel Schriftman and Sol Kone are arrested for the attempted bribe of Victoria Price.

1935

APRIL 1: The United States Supreme Court reverses the convictions of Norris and Patterson, on the grounds that Negroes were excluded from the panels of the grand and petit jurors who indicted and convicted them.

MAY 1: Victoria Price swears out new warrants against all nine defendants.

NOVEMBER 13: A special grand jury is called at Scottsboro. For the first time since Reconstruction, a black man sits on an Alabama jury. All nine prisoners are indicted for rape once again.

1936

JANUARY 1: The defendants, except for the two juveniles, are arraigned and plead not guilty.

JANUARY 23: Haywood Patterson is convicted and his punishment is fixed at seventy-five years in prison.

JANUARY 24: The trials of Clarence Norris and the remaining five adult defendants are postponed pending Patterson's appeal. Ozie Powell attacks Deputy Sheriff Edgar Blalock and is shot in the head by Sheriff Jay Sandlin.

1937

JUNE 14: The Alabama Supreme Court upholds the conviction of Haywood Patterson.

JULY 15: Clarence Norris is convicted and sentenced to death in the electric chair.

JULY 22: Andy Wright is sentenced to ninety-nine years.

JULY 24: Charlie Weems receives seventy-five years. The rape charge against Ozie Powell is dropped. He is convicted of assault on a deputy sheriff and given twenty years.

JULY 24: All charges are dropped against Roy Wright, Eugene Williams, Olen Montgomery and Willie Roberson. They are released.

JULY 26: Clarence Norris is returned to the death house at Kilby Prison. Charlie Weems, Ozie Powell and Andy Wright also are sent to Kilby Prison. Haywood Patterson is incarcerated in the Atmore Prison Farm.

OCTOBER 26: The United States Supreme Court declines to review the convictions of Haywood Patterson and Clarence Norris.

1938

JUNE 16: The Alabama Supreme Court affirms the death sentence of Clarence Norris and orders him to be put to death on August 19, 1938.

JULY 5: Governor Bibb Graves commutes Clarence Norris' sentence to life imprisonment.

AUGUST 20: Roy Wright, Eugene Williams, Olen Montgomery and Willie Roberson appear onstage at Harlem's Apollo Theatre as a "Special Added Attraction."

1939-1942

The Scottsboro Defense Committee negotiates with prominent Alabama citizens for assistance in gaining freedom for the five men still imprisoned.

1943

NOVEMBER 17:   Charlie Weems is paroled.

1944

JANUARY 6:   Clarence Norris and Andy Wright are released on parole.

SEPTEMBER 27:   Norris and Wright leave Alabama in violation of their paroles.

OCTOBER 18:   Clarence Norris is returned to Kilby Prison.

1946

SEPTEMBER 27:   Ozie Powell is released on parole; Clarence Norris gets another parole.

SEPTEMBER 30:   Clarence Norris is declared a parole delinquent when he leaves Alabama once again.

1947

FEBRUARY 7:   Andy Wright is released for a brief period but returned to prison when his employer discovers he is a Scottsboro Boy and fires him.

1948

JULY 17:   Haywood Patterson escapes.

1950

JUNE 9:   Andy Wright is the last defendant to leave

the Alabama prisons permanently. He has a job in Albany, New York.

DECEMBER 18: Haywood Patterson kills a black man in Detroit, Michigan.

1951

JULY 12: Andy Wright is found innocent of the rape of a thirteen-year-old girl.

SEPTEMBER 25: Haywood Patterson is found guilty of manslaughter and sentenced to fifteen to twenty years in the Michigan state prison.

1952

AUGUST 24: Haywood Patterson dies of lung cancer.

1953

MAY: Clarence Norris moves to New York City.

1959

AUGUST 17: Roy Wright stabs his wife to death in a jealous rage, then commits suicide.

1970

DECEMBER: The NAACP agrees to help Clarence Norris get his parole violation lifted or obtain a pardon.

1974

OCTOBER 10: The Alabama Board of Pardons and Paroles insists that Norris must return to Alabama to have his case considered. He declines.

1976

AUGUST 5: The attorney general of Alabama sends a letter to the pardons and paroles board stating that in his opinion, based on research and study of the case, Clarence Norris is innocent of the 1931 rape charges and is due a pardon.

OCTOBER 25: Governor George Wallace approves the pardon of Clarence Norris and he is unconditionally freed.

Appendix

The documents in the appendix bridge the history of the Alabama prison system and of the Scottsboro Case from 1927 to the present day. The lists, letters, and prison forms give an overall view of the bureaucracy that determined the fate of Clarence Norris.

The following list is in chronological sequence by year, month, date, name, race, sex, county of conviction, offense and the name of the Governor who was in office at the time of the electrocution, of the electrocutions performed at Kilby Prison, Montgomery, Alabama.

NO.	YEAR MONTH	NAME	RS	COUNTY	OFFENSE	GOVERNOR
1.	1927 April 8	DeVAUGHAN, Horace	CM	Jefferson	Murder	Graves
2.	1927 April 23	MURPHY, W. Virgil	WM	Houston	Murder	Graves
3.	1927 July 15	BACHELOR, Clyde R.	WM	Elmore	Murder	Graves
4.	1927 Sept 9	HALL, Sam	CM	Autauga	Murder	Graves
5.	1927 Dec 16	COLEMAN Jeff	CM	Jefferson	Murder	Graves
6.	1927 Dec 30	EATMAN, Bob	CM	Hale	Murder	Graves
7.	1928 March 9	BURCHFIELD, John	WM	Chambers	Murder	Graves
8.	1928 March 9	WASHINGTON, Charlie	CM	Jefferson	Murder	Graves

Appendix

NO.	YEAR MONTH	NAME	RS COUNTY	OFFENSE	GOVERNOR
9.	1928 April 6	BROOKS, Isiah	CM Crenshaw	Murder	Graves
10.	1928 June 15	SHELTON, Robert	CM Mobile	Murder	Graves
11.	1928 July 10	PEOPLES, Rodel	CM Jefferson	Murder	Graves
12.	1929 March 15	JILES, Dock	CM Lee	Murder	Graves
13.	1929 July 26	CARTER, Will	CM −	Murder	Graves
14.	1929 Aug 23	HARRIS, Charles	CM Barbour	Murder	Graves
15.	1930 Jan 24	GILMORE, Silena	CF Jefferson	Murder	Graves
16.	1930 March 14	JARVIS, Jack	WM Mobile	Murder	Graves
17.	1930 June 20	BROWN, Jack	CM Marengo	Murder	Graves
18.	1930 June 20	HARRIS, Edgar	CM Marengo	Murder	Graves
19.	1930 June 20	MILES, Roy Lee	CM Bullock	Murder	Graves
20.	1931 Feb 27	MALONE, Cleveland	CM Talladega	Rape	Miller
21.	1931 March 11	IRVIN, Percy	CM Lowndes	Robbery	Miller
22.	1931 March 11	MIMS, Isaac	CM Lowndes	Murder	Miller
23.	1931 March 27	DANIELS, Moses	CM Montgomery	Rape	Miller
24.	1931 May 29	BATES, Spencer	CM Sumter	Murder	Miller
25.	1931 July 10	HOKES, William	CM St. Clair	Murder	Miller
26.	1932 Jan 15	WILLIAMS, Charley	CM Mobile	Rape	Miller
27.	1932 Jan 15	ASHE, Richard	CM Hale	Murder	Miller
28.	1932 Feb 3	JOHNSON, Willie J.	CM Jefferson	Murder	Miller
29.	1932 Feb 3	JONES, Charlie	CM Jefferson	Murder	Miller
30.	1933 March 22	RUFF, Blake	CM Clay	Murder	Miller
31.	1933 Oct 27	MEADOWS, George	CM Montgomery	Robbery	Miller
32.	1934 Feb 9	FOSTER, Bennie	CM Dallas	Murder	Miller
33.	1934 Feb 9	THOMPSON, John	CM Mobile	Murder	Miller
34.	1934 Feb 9	WHITE, Harie	CM Mobile	Murder	Miller
35.	1934 Feb 9	WALLER, Ernest	CM Dallas	Murder	Miller
36.	1934 Feb 9	ROPER, Solomon	CM Dallas	Murder	Miller
37.	1934 March 1	THOMAS, Ed	CM Hale	Murder	Miller
38.	1936 Feb 21	PRESTON, Johny	CM Lee	Murder	Graves
39.	1936 March 20	ROPER, Eddie	CM Jefferson	Murder	Graves
40.	1936 March 20	DUDLEY, Robert	CM Jefferson	Murder	Graves
41.	1936 March 27	PETERSON, Henry	CM Montgomery	Murder	Graves
42.	1936 April 17	BYNUM, Willie E.	CM Montgomery	Murder	Graves
43.	1936 May 5	GAST, Joseph W.	WM Tuscaloosa	Murder	Graves
44.	1936 May 15	COSEY, Waddie	CM Morgan	Murder	Graves
45.	1936 May 15	STEWART, Jimmie	CM Montgomery	Murder	Graves
46.	1936 June 12	VINCENT, Wesley	WM Jefferson	Murder	Graves
47.	1936 June 12	HARRELL, Tyrie	CM Elmore	Murder	Graves
48.	1936 June 12	WATERS, Gabel	CM Sumter	Murder	Graves
49.	1936 June 19	ARARANT, Elmer N.	WM Lowndes	Murder	Graves

Appendix

NO.	YEAR MONTH	NAME	RS	COUNTY	OFFENSE	GOVERNOR
50.	1936 June 19	MILLER, Walter	CM	Madison	Murder	Graves
51.	1936 July 3	PERKINS, Tomy	CM	Monroe	Murder	Graves
52.	1936 July 10	SMILEY, A. B.	CM	Elmore	Murder	Graves
53.	1936 July 31	PATTERSON, Oscar	CM	Coosa	Carnal K.	Graves
54.	1936 Aug 7	SUMMERVILLE, Ed Lee	CM	Pickens	Murder	Graves
55.	1937 Jan 29	SKELTON, Edgar Prude	WM	Tuscaloosa	Murder	Graves
56.	1937 Feb 26	FRANKLIN, James Victor	WM	Tuscaloosa	Murder	Graves
57.	1937 June 11	COLLINS, Roosevelt	CM	Calhoun	Rape	Graves
58.	1937 Sept 10	OLIVER, Arthur	WM	Elmore	Murder	Graves
59.	1938 Jan 28	MILLHOUSE, Frank	CM	Mobile	Murder	Graves
60.	1938 Jan 28	VAUGHAN, R. P.	CM	Mobile	Murder	Graves
61.	1938 July 22	DAVIDSON, Mack	CM	Baldwin	Robbery	Graves
62.	1938 July 22	YOUNG, Gary	CM	Mobile	Murder	Graves
63.	1938 Aug 19	COBB, Curtis	CM	Jefferson	Rape	Graves
64.	1938 Aug 19	WHITFIELD, Willie J.	CM	Montgomery	Murder	Graves
65.	1938 Nov 25	VAUGHAN, Connie	WM	Jefferson	Murder	Graves
66.	1938 Nov 25	BROWN, Jimmie	CM	Jefferson	Rape	Graves
67.	1938 Dec 30	SMITH, Adolph	CM	Geneva	Robbery	Graves
68.	1939 Feb 17	WARE, Fred	CM	Randolph	Rape	Dixon
69.	1939 March 17	WIMBUSH, Edward	CM	Jefferson	Murder	Dixon
70.	1939 March 17	KENNEDY, Joe Lee	CM	Jefferson	Murder	Dixon
71.	1939 April 14	WILLIAMS, Tom	CM	Elmore	Murder	Dixon
72.	1939 June 9	ANDERSON, Ray	CM	Jefferson	Rape	Dixon
73.	1939 June 9	FRAZIER, John	CM	Marengo	Murder	Dixon
74.	1939 June 9	TUBBS, Grady	CM	Hale	Murder	Dixon
75.	1939 June 9	WHITE, Charles	CM	Pike	Rape	Dixon
76.	1939 July 7	SANDERS, Robert	CM	Montgomery	Murder	Dixon
77.	1939 Aug 18	JACKSON, Mack	CM	Jefferson	Rape	Dixon
78.	1940 Feb 16	TUCKER, Calvin	CM	Mobile	Murder	Dixon
79.	1940 March 15	AVERY, Lonnie	CM	Bibb	Murder	Dixon
80.	1940 March 29	BELL, Herman	CM	Mobile	Rape	Dixon
81.	1940 March 29	JACKSON, Mack	CM	Jefferson	Murder	Dixon
82.	1940 March 29	WILLIAMS, David	CM	Jefferson	Murder	Dixon
83.	1940 May 3	RAGLAND, Judge	CM	Lee	Murder	Dixon
84.	1940 May 24	MCGUIRE, David	CM	Jefferson	Murder	Dixon
85.	1940 June 14	WILLIAMS, Willie C.	WM	Jefferson	Murder	Dixon
86.	1940 Aug 9	BRANDON, Willie James	CM	Coffee	Rape	Dixon
87.	1941 Jan 17	CLARK, William	CM	Limestone	Rape	Dixon
88.	1941 July 11	JACKSON, Julius	CM	Talladega	Murder	Dixon
89.	1941 Aug 8	JONES, Robert	CM	Greene	Murder	Dixon
90.	1941 Aug 8	BASS, Frank	CM	Morgan	Burglary	Dixon

Appendix

NO.	YEAR MONTH	NAME	RS COUNTY	OFFENSE	GOVERNOR
91.	1942 Jan 9	DYER, Albert	WM Jefferson	Murder	Dixon
92.	1942 Jan 23	POWELL, Dock	CM Clay	Murder	Dixon
93.	1942 March 13	GIPSON, Esker W.	WM Mobile	Murder	Dixon
94.	1942 March 13	HERRING, Bud Phelps	CM Coffee	Murder	Dixon
95.	1942 May 1	HARDY, Clarence	CM Jefferson	Murder	Dixon
96.	1942 May 1	HAYES, Ed Jr.	CM Marengo	Murder	Dixon
97.	1942 June 26	PATTERSON, William M.	CM Jefferson	Murder	Dixon
98.	1942 June 26	SNEAD, William Nelms	CM Jefferson	Rape	Dixon
99.	1942 July 10	MEALER, Paul	WM Tuscaloosa	Murder	Dixon
100.	1943 Feb 19	BASSIE, Haywood	CM Marengo	Murder	Sparks
101.	1943 June 4	JOHNSON, Frank	CM Jefferson	Rape	Sparks
102.	1943 Aug 6	GOLDSMITH, Leroy	CM Montgomery	Murder	Sparks
103.	1943 Aug 13	DANIELS, Henry Jr.	CM Mobile	Rape	Sparks
104.	1943 Aug 13	ROBINSON, Curtis	CM Mobile	Rape	Sparks
105.	1944 March 24	MITCHELL, Lewis	CM Montgomery	Murder	Sparks
106.	1944 Nov 3	VERNON, Joe	CM Jefferson	Murder	Sparks
107.	1945 March 16	HOCKENBERRY, Joseph H.	WM Jefferson	Rape	Sparks
108.	1945 March 16	REEDY, Daniel F.	WM Jefferson	Rape	Sparks
109.	1945 July 20	PATTON, Ed Lucky	CM Hale	Murder	Sparks
110.	1946 Jan 18	HALL, Peter Paul	CM Barbour	Murder	Sparks
111.	1946 Jan 25	JOHNSON, Ernest	CM Hale	Murder	Sparks
112.	1946 Feb 1	BROWN, Richard	CM Hale	Murder	Sparks
113.	1946 March 15	BURNS, Elbert J.	WM Jefferson	Murder	Sparks
114.	1946 April 19	PILLEY, Robert S.	WM Jefferson	Murder	Sparks
115.	1946 May 24	WINGARD, Lester	CM Montgomery	Murder	Sparks
116.	1946 May 24	HICKS, Fred	CM Hale	Murder	Sparks
117.	1946 June 14	MINCEY, Joe	CM Pike	Murder	Sparks
118.	1946 Aug 16	ALSTON, William Edgar	WM Walker	Murder	Sparks
119.	1946 Dec 13	SMITH, Johnie B.	CM Tuscaloosa	Rape	Sparks
120.	1947 March 14	BROOKS, Booker T.	CM Chambers	Murder	Folsom
121.	1947 May 23	GARRETT, Israel	CM Russell	Murder	Folsom
122.	1948 March 19	GRANT, Noel J.	WM Baldwin	Murder	Folsom
123.	1948 March 19	MUNSON, John Henry Jr.	CM Jefferson	Murder	Folsom
124.	1949 March 11	COBB, Phillip	CM Montgomery	Murder	Folsom
125.	1949 March 18	HAYGOOD, Perry Lee	CM Jefferson	Murder	Folsom
126.	1949 March 25	SNEAD, Buster	CM Bibb	Murder	Folsom
127.	1949 Aug 12	GREEN, Nehemiah	CM Jefferson	Murder	Folsom
128.	1949 Aug 12	WINTERS, J. C.	CM Elmore	Murder	Folsom
129.	1950 May 26	SMITH, Charlie	CM Mobile	Murder	Folsom
130.	1950 July 21	KEITH, Joe	CM Limestone	Murder	Folsom
131.	1950 July 21	ODOM, Homer Garland	WM Jefferson	Murder	Folsom
132.	1950 July 21	SIMS, Claude B.	CM Jefferson	Murder	Folsom

Appendix

NO.	YEAR MONTH	NAME	RS COUNTY	OFFENSE	GOVERNOR
133.	1952 May 2	DRAKE, Cooper	CM Shelby	Murder	Persons
134.	1952 May 2	SMITH, Andrew Lee	CM Jefferson	Murder	Persons
135.	1952 May 9	FORREST, Leverett	CM Mobile	Murder	Persons
136.	1952 Oct 10	MILES, Desmond	WM Covington	Murder	Persons
137.	1953 Aug 28	MYHAUD, Reuben	CM Geneva	Rape	Persons
138.	1953 Sept 4	DENNISON, Earle	WF Elmore	Murder	Persons
139.	1954 Jan 22	HARDY, Will	CM Tuscaloosa	Murder	Persons
140.	1954 April 23	JONES, Albert Lee	CM Russell	Murder	Persons
141.	1954 April 23	GRIMES, Arthur Lee	CM Russell	Murder	Persons
142.	1954 June 4	JACKSON, Jessie Frank	CM Montgomery	Rape	Persons
143.	1956 Sept 28	JACKSON, Melvin	CM Russell	Rape	Folsom
144.	1957 March 22	JOHNSON, Clarence	CM Wilcox	Murder	Folsom
145.	1957 Oct 11	MARTIN, Rhonda Bell	WF Montgomery	Murder	Folsom
146.	1958 March 28	REEVES, Jeremiah	CM Montgomery	Rape	Folsom
147.	1959 Dec 4	WALKER, Ernest Cornell	CM Jefferson	Rape	Patterson
148.	1959 Dec 11	DOCKERY, Edwin Ray	WM Morgan	Murder	Patterson
149.	1960 April 29	BOGGS, Columbus	CM Dallas	Murder	Patterson
150.	1961 Nov 24	JOHNSON, Joe Henry	CM Limestone	Murder	Patterson
151.	1962 Aug 31	GOSA, Wilmon	CM Tuscaloosa	Murder	Patterson
152.	1964 Sept 4	COBERN, James W.	WM Dallas	Robbery	Wallace
153.	1965 Jan 15	BOWEN, William F. Jr.	WM Madison	Murder	Wallace

[This letter was written by Walter White, then executive director of the NAACP, in his initial efforts to help the Scottsboro defendants.]

THE THOMAS JEFFERSON HOTEL
BIRMINGHAM, ALABAMA

5 May 1931

DEAR HERB AND BOB:

Things begin to look a bit better though we're far from being out of the woods. Yesterday I inveigled the Rev. Terrell (who was scared to death) to go with me to Kilby Prison at Montgomery. After hours of red tape unwinding we got into Death Row with the warden (whose name appropriately enough is Walls), two deputy wardens, and a turnkey hovering over my shoulder while I talked to the boys. More of that—it is a long and exciting story—when I get back. I got four boys to sign an agreement, two others want to write their parents first for advice, and the other two want to stick with the I.L.D.

One thing is certain—no I.L.D. representative will ever get in to to see them! Today I talked with Roderick Beddow, the best criminal lawyer in Birmingham and who, though only forty or so, is the Darrow of this part of the country. He is a fighter and everybody agrees that if he will take the case, he can do more than any other lawyer in the country. He is interested, declares the whole trial an outrage, and will take the case. I have ordered a transcript for him by wire and he is going this weekend to Kilby to talk with the boys.

I have just come from a long and highly satisfactory talk with the editor and managing editor of the *Post*, Scripps Howard paper. The editor used to be on the

World and called me a number of times, he tells me, about stories. They believed the boys guilty but now are openminded and are going to keep us tipped off on all developments. Hollace Ransdall, the Civil Liberties investigator, arrives this afternoon and I am suggesting to her that she set out tomorrow for Scottsboro and Huntsville (the two "raped" girls live there) to see what she can dig up there. Am off tonight for Atlanta where the parents of four of the boys live to see what I can do about getting them straightened out.

Will see you Friday morning about ten thirty.

BROADWAY TABERNACLE CHURCH
BROADWAY AND FIFTY-SIXTH STREET
NEW YORK

CHARLES E. JEFFERSON
Honorary Minister

ALLAN KNIGHT CHALMERS
Minister

FRANK W. MURTFELDT
Associate Pastor

CORRELIA G. WICKS
Parish Visitor

MARION L. NORRIS
Minister's Secretary

January 9, 1937

DEAR ALLAN:

Your letter just here (Thurs. P.M. Oakland air special). OK about Committee. Frances just gave me juicy bits from your letters to her.

So sorry arrangements are not complete! Thought you would remain at Oakland, but sent letter yesterday to International House at Berkeley, with enclosures. WILL YOU ASK TO HAVE IT FORWARDED TO YOU? PLEASE? Also Frances wrote there.

Letter from Arthur Keimel, Mittineague Church, West Springfield, saying he had resigned to take effect July first. He sends copy of resignation in local paper, and asks if you can help him to find an opening. Mention it in case you run across something.

Shapiro just phoned. They saw Leibowitz yesterday, and went over the whole situation very carefully.

1. Leibowitz says a shorter sentence is absolutely out of the question; that these terms were arrived at after considerable argument, question, etc.

2. The question of Patterson will have to remain a question of trust. He was told that Governor Graves will take care of this before he goes out of office. He (Leibowitz) says that they must take some chance on this thing. He is convinced that Carmichael is doing things in good faith.

264

3. Nothing can be done about Powell. They are merely going to try him, but cannot tell how long a sentence he will get.

Leibowitz wants the SDC to get together and draw up a statement to be signed by each one of the committee stating their views of the whole thing so that he can have it clearly before him.

Shapiro is asking Norman Thomas to draw up such a statement for the committee. Probably on Monday it will be ready and will be sent to you air special (This means to Oakland.) I imagine they will get your approval before having the others sign it.

Everything OK here. Frank is preaching on LONELI-NESS tomorrow.

Our best to you, "Mutt and Jeff!"

As ever
MARION

[This letter was written by Ruby Bates to her boyfriend.]

Jan 5, 1933
Huntsville, Ala.
215 Connelly Ave.

DEAREST EARL,

I want to make a statement too you Mary Sanders is a goddam lie about those Negroes jazzing me those policemen made me tell a lie that is my statement because I want to clear myself that is all too if you want to believe me OK. If not that is okay. You will be sorry someday if you had too stay in jail with eight Negroes you would tell a lie two those Negroes did not touch me or those white boys I hope you will believe me they dont, i love you better than Mary does or anybody else in the world that is why I am telling you of this thing. i was drunk at the time and did not know what i was doing i know it was wrong too let those Negroes die on account of me i hope you will believe my statement because it is the gods truth i hope you will believe me i was jazzed but those white boys jazzed me i wish those Negroes are not Burnt on account of me it is those white boys fault that is my statement, and that is all I know i hope you tell the law hope you will answer.

RUBY BATES

Huntsville Ala
215 Connelly Ave.
P.S. This is one time that I might tell a lie But it is the truth so God help me.

[This telegram was sent by Forney Johnston, a prominent Birmingham attorney and the son of a former governor. He is writing Dr. Allan Knight Chalmers to explain why Governor Graves did not pardon the defendants as he had promised.]

RECEIVED AT 955 EIGHTH AVE. NEW YORK
BH408 201 DL = BIRMINGHAM ALA 14 306P
DR ALLEN KNIGHT CHALMERS
BWAY TABERNACLE CHURCH BWAY AND 56 ST
CONFIDENTIAL TO YOU AND ASSOCIATES. EARNEST TALK WITH GOVERNOR WITHOUT EFFECT. DISORDER LAST WEEK ARISING OUT OF SIMILAR CHARGE CONVINCES HIM THAT ACTION SHOULD NOT BE DELAYED. THIS MADE IT NECESSARY FOR ME TO MENTION THE SUGGESTION OF YOUR LETTER. HE UNDERSTANDS THEIR INTEREST AND DESIRE TO TALK WITH HIM IF CONSISTENT WITH HIS PUBLIC DUTY BUT APPEARS FOR SOME REASON UNDER TREMENDOUS PRESSURE TO ACT NOW, AND ADVISED ME THAT HE WOULD MARK THE APPLICATION DENIED TOMORROW. NOTHING CAN STOP THIS UNLESS POSSIBLY TELEPHONE FROM PARTY YOU TALKED WITH TO MRS. GRAVES. I HAVE IMPRESSION THAT IF HE IS RELIEVED OF THE IMMEDIATE PRESSURE BY MARKING APPLICATION DENIED IT MAY YET BE REVIVED BEFORE END OF HIS TERM BY ADVANCING THE PAROLE ARRANGEMENTS AS IF A NEW PROPOSAL, BUT OF COURSE THAT IS A BARE AND UNSATISFACTORY POSSIBILITY. I URGED HIM TO GIVE CONSIDERATION TO PUBLIC STATEMENT OF THE NATURE DISCUSSED, BUT SENSED THAT WHATEVER IS INDUCING HIS CONCLUSION IS SO PRESSING THAT HE DOES NOT WANT TO BE SWAYED. DEEPLY REGRET THIS APPARENTLY FINAL ACTION. HE WILL MAKE NO ADVERSE STATEMENT IN DENYING APPLICATION. HE SEEMS TO ME SINCERE IN BELIEVING THAT PRISONERS ARE DETERMINED UPON DISORDER IF RELEASED.

F.J.

[This letter from Carroll Kilpatrick to the Scottsboro Defense Committee secretary Morris Shapiro is his effort to give requested advice on how to deal with the Alabama Parole Board for the best results. Kilpatrick is a native of Alabama and had been a well-known newspaper reporter with the Birmingham *News*. A Neiman Fellow at Harvard when he wrote this letter, he went on to become the White House correspondent for the Washington *Post*.]

B-35 Adams House
Cambridge, Massachusetts
March 13, 1940

Mr. Morris Shapiro
225 Broadway
New York, New York

DEAR MORRIS:

I am afraid I can't give you any advice at all regarding the tactics to be used with the Parole Board. I frankly don't know what could be done. My first reaction on reading the decision was that the gloves should be taken off and the idiots who run the State of Alabama shown up to the people. They would really make Machiavelli look naive.

One thought I had was that the whole story should be told from beginning to end; I mean the story of the last two or three years. I hope that you are saving all your correspondence with complete notes and some day will give me permission to publish it. What about an article now for the NEW REPUBLIC, or would that do any good? Would it be possible to discuss procedure with Mr. Justice Black? It seems to me that the Committee has been as honest and fair with the officials in Montgomery as it is possible to have been. If you can get somewhere now by exposing them, or conducting a vigorous open campaign, I think you are fully justified in doing so. I hate to see the state humiliated again, but it seems to me it has already humiliated itself beyond repair.

I mentioned in a note the other day to Mr. Chappell my dismay over the decision. Perhaps he will write in full his reaction. His advice I think you should get. At least you might have it before taking any action.

The other day we had Henry L. Mencken to dinner, and he remarked casually he had never known an honest politician. Apparently he shocked one of the group who challenged him. Mencken replied, "I will go further. Not only have I never known an honest politician, but I have never heard of one, and if there had been one I am sure someone would have told me about him. I have always been interested in curiosities."

It looks as though you have been led out on a limb. You were given definite assurance that if you dropped the case in court, action would be taken by the governor.

I would like very much to know what you are going to do.

Yours very sincerely,
KILPATRICK

ALABAMA
STATE BOARD OF ADJUSTMENT
MONTGOMERY

MEMBERS:
A.R. FORSYTH,
 CHAIRMAN
JOHN BRANDON,
 SECRETARY
CHAS. E. McCALL,
 STATE TREASURER

Special Attorney
Files Crenshaw

January 14, 1943

Clarence Norris
Kilby Prison
Montgomery, Ala.

DEAR CLARENCE:

This will acknowledge receipt of your letter of the 12th with reference to the accident in which you lost a finger in 1939.

Our records disclose that you filed a claim on October 31, 1939, for the loss of a forefinger and that on March 5, 1940, the claim was denied.

Yours very truly,

JOHN BRANDON
Secretary

Bab

THE CITY OF NEW YORK
OFFICE OF THE
PRESIDENT OF THE BOROUGH OF MANHATTAN
NEW YORK, N.Y. 10007

PERCY E. SUTTON
PRESIDENT

June 21, 1976

Mr. Roy Wilkins
Executive Director
National Association for the Advancement
of Colored People
1790 Broadway
New York, N.Y. 10019

Re: Willie Norris

DEAR MR. WILKINS:

I am pleased to join with other officials and citizens of the State and City of New York in endorsing your efforts on behalf of Willie Norris.

The record which Mr. Norris has compiled as a responsible citizen, a good worker and family man, speaks eloquently; and in my view his continued residence in New York would be in the best interests of society.

There is no doubt, now, that a egregious miscarriage of justice occurred in the cases of the "Scottsboro Boys." While the wrongs cannot be fully righted, I feel that the least we can do is to help to give Mr. Norris, the only surviving Scottsboro defendant, some peace of mind at this period of his life through an effort at securing him a pardon at this time.

271

You have my permission to convey these sentiments to officials of the State of Alabama.

Very truly yours,

PERCY E. SUTTON

THE CITY OF NEW YORK
OFFICE OF THE MAYOR
NEW YORK, N.Y. 10007

June 25, 1976

Mr. Roy Wilkins
Executive Director
National Association for the Advancement
  of Colored People
1790 Broadway
New York, New York 10019

DEAR ROY:

I want to take this opportunity to thank you for bringing to my attention the case of Clarence Norris, the last of the Scottsboro defendants.

The story of Mr. Norris and his co-defendants is, of course, one of the great human tragedies of our time. It is a compelling case that meets every criterion for the ideal we hold most dear in our criminal justice system: justice tempered with mercy.

From the information conveyed to me through your good offices, I find exemplary cause for an exceptional gesture of humanitarianism and compassion. I am therefore, pleased to join with you in urging the Governor of Alabama to grant a pardon to Clarence Norris in the interests of justice and decency. It is clear that Mr. Norris who, as you so pertinently note, has been a law-abiding citizen of our City for 23 years, has paid his debt to society and that he and his family are entitled to have this matter closed once and for all so that they can live out their lives in the serenity and dignity they have earned and deserve.

I am proud to be counted among the many concerned

citizens who support this most worthy cause and I earnestly hope that our efforts will be successful.

With warmest regards, I am

Sincerely,

ABRAHAM D. BEAME
M A Y O R

UNITED STATES SENATE

WASHINGTON, D.C. 20510

JACOB K. JAVITS
NEW YORK

COMMITTEES:
LABOR AND PUBLIC WELFARE
FOREIGN RELATIONS
GOVERNMENT OPERATIONS
JOINT ECONOMIC
SMALL BUSINESS

REGIONAL OFFICES:
ROOM 511
110 EAST 45th STREET
NEW YORK, NEW YORK 10017
ROOM 222
FEDERAL OFFICE BUILDING
111 WEST HURON STREET
BUFFALO, NEW YORK 14202
ROOM, 420
LEO W. O'BRIEN FEDERAL
BUILDING
CLINTON SQUARE
ALBANY, NEW YORK 12207

September 20, 1976

DEAR MEMBERS OF THE BOARD:

I understand that the case of Mr. Clarence Norris may be considered by the Board in the near future. The long history of litigation and public commentary concerning this case constitutes an extraordinary record of social and political history, as well as a legal odyssey almost unique in our time.

Although I am not personally familiar with Mr. Norris or the facts developed in the episode known as the "Scottsboro Case," I have been advised that Mr. Norris spent almost 15 years of his life in prison, despite the fact that substantial evidence existed that he was not guilty of the crimes charged.

Having been tried three times, and with the United States Supreme Court reversing the conviction of Mr. Norris and his codefendants on the ground that black citizens had been illegally excluded from trial juries, Mr. Norris ought now to be granted the long delayed justice which was not done in his case.

I respectfully suggest to the Board that it act affirmatively, particularly in view of the fact that Mr.

275

Norris has lived a useful and productive life in New York City and, at the age of 64 finally ought to have this matter resolved.

Sincerely,

Jacob K. Javits

Board of Pardons and Paroles
State of Alabama
654 Administrative Building
Montgomery, Alabama 36130

STATE OF ALABAMA
BOARD OF PARDONS AND PAROLES
MONTGOMERY, ALABAMA 36130

NORMAN F. USSERY
Chairman of the Board
WILLIAM R. ROBINSON
Member of the Board
SARA COUSINS SELLERS
Member of the Board

DAVID H. WILLIAMS
Executive Director

October 22, 1976

Mr. Clarence Norris #39,745
2676 Linden Boulevard
New York, New York
DEAR MR. NORRIS:

On this date Board Members Mrs. Sara Cousins Sellers
and William R. Robinson voted to void the delinquency
taken in your case on September 30, 1976, and reinstate
you on parole but without supervision. We have further
ordered that you be granted a Conditional Release from
supervision.

This action was taken based on information from the
State of New York that you have lived there for the past
30 years, have worked regularly and have now become a
useful citizen. We feel that in view of this it would not be
necessary to place you under supervision at this time.

Sincerely yours,

WILLIAM R. ROBINSON
Member of the Board

WRR/dl

THE ATTORNEY GENERAL
STATE OF ALABAMA/MONTGOMERY, ALABAMA 36130

WILLIAM J. BAXLEY
Attorney General
GEORGE L. BECK
Deputy Attorney General
E. RAY ACTON
Executive Assistant
WALTER S. TURNER
Chief Assistant Attorney General
LUCY M. RICHARDS
Confidential Assistant
JACK D. SHOWS
Chief Investigator

October 25, 1976

Board of Pardons and Paroles
State of Alabama
654 Administrative Building
Montgomery, Alabama, 36130

DEAR MEMBERS OF THE BOARD:

In my August 5, 1976 letter to you, I briefly chronicled the case of Clarence Norris, a defendant in the case commonly known as the "Scottsboro Case." I stated at that time my belief based on the facts of the case, that Clarence Norris was and is innocent of the crime for which he stands convicted.

Clarence Norris was tried on three separate occasions on the charge of rape. At each trial the evidence and testimony of the witnesses were substantially the same, with the significant exception that one of the alleged rape victims, Ruby Bates, retracted her testimony after the first trial, admitted she had perjured herself and that there was no rape.

Victoria Price, the remaining prosecutrix, testified at the last trial of Clarence Norris that she was raped by

Clarence Norris and the eight other defendants. Pertinent excerpts of her testimony are as follows:

—Price stated she was brutally raped on a railroad freight car containing chert, a rocky, pebblelike substance.

—The attack was violent in that she was struck on the head with the butt of a pistol causing bleeding.

—Each attacker, over eight in number, sexually penetrated her and ejaculated causing semen to be present not only in and on her genitals but also on her clothing.

—The attackers beat her severely about the head and face, bruising and scratching her extensively throughout her body causing pronounced swelling of her nose, lips, ankles and bleeding.

—Price testified that the mass rape resulted in bleeding from the vagina.

The time lapse between the alleged rape and the examination of Victoria Price by Dr. Bridges and Dr. Lynch was within approximately two hours of the alleged rape according to the record. The testimony of Dr. Bridges, the physician who examined Victoria Price, revealed the following pertinent facts.

—Dr. Bridges testified that he did not find any wound on the head of Victoria Price which might conceivably have been caused by a blow of a weapon.

—Dr. Bridges saw no blood on her scalp nor did Price complain of any head injury or blood on the scalp.

—Dr. Bridges states he found only some small scratches on the wrist and back of Price. There were no lacerations or bleeding as claimed by Price.

—From testimony it appears that Victoria Price had been traveling, prior to the alleged incident, on freight trains and living in camps among the hobos.

—The physicians during their examination did not find any signs of fresh semen on Victoria Price's genital organs nor on her clothing as she claims.

279

—Whatever substance was found resembling semen was present on Price's body long before the alleged rape by Clarence Norris, according to the testimony of Dr. Bridges.

—Testimony revealed that Victoria Price had engaged in sexual intercourse sometime prior to boarding the train containing Clarence Norris and his companions.

—Dr. Bridges' examination confirmed that there was no blood being emitted from Price's vagina as she claimed nor did her genitals appear bruised or ripped as Price claimed.

—The doctor observed the physical appearance and demeanor of Victoria Price during her physical examination and Dr. Bridges testified that Price was neither hysterical nor appeared nervous. The doctor noted that her respiration and pulse were normal, a state incompatible with a rape victim.

It appears clearly from the physical examination of Victoria Price that there was no evidence of a brutal, massive rape and that the statements made by Victoria Price in regard to Clarence Norris, are totally unworthy of belief.

As observed by Judge Horton in his opinion on the evidence, the same evidence and testimony presented at the trial which convicted Clarence Norris, the law mandates that a person not be convicted of rape absent corroboration, particularly where the testimony of the prosecutrix bears as in this case blatant conflicts and lacks any support from scientific evidence.

Based on the scientific evaluation of the physician who examined Victoria Price, it is impossible that she was raped as she alleged.

For the reasons stated above, I again vigorously appeal to this board to review all the evidence in this case and swiftly grant to Clarence Norris a full and complete pardon. Mr. Norris will continue to live a nightmare until this board removes from him the unjust stigma of conviction for a crime which the overwhelming evidence clearly shows he did not commit.

Sincerely,
BILL BAXLEY
Attorney General
By—

BB/sa

MILTON C. DAVIS
Assistant Attorney General